The Enigmatic Samuel Aughey:

Nebraska's Pastor Naturalist

Hugh H. Genoways

Margaret R. Bolick

Mary Anne Andrei

Zea Books
Lincoln, Nebraska
2025

ISBN 978-1-60962-345-6   paperback
ISBN 978-1-60962-346-3 electronic book

Composed in Palatino Linotype.

Digital ebook edition (pdf) available at
http://digitalcommons.unl.edu
Print edition available from
http://www.lulu.com/spotlight/unllib

Cover Image: Photograph of Samuel Aughey taken in 1871. Courtesy of Erwin H. Barbour, Museum Photographs Series (RG 32-01-01). Archives & Special Collections, University of Nebraska–Lincoln Libraries.
Cover design: Paul Royster

Contents

The Authors

Hugh H. Genoways
University of Nebraska State Museum,
University of Nebraska-Lincoln,
Lincoln, Nebraska 68588 USA
Correspondence: h.h.genoways@gmail.com

Margaret R. Bolick
Division of Research & Economic Development,
North Carolina A&T State University,
1601 E. Market Street,
Greensboro, North Carolina 27411 USA

Mary Anne Andrei
Department of Media Studies,
Oliphant Hall, Room 128,
University of Tulsa,
Tulsa, OK 74104 USA

Abstract

Samuel Aughey at age 39 became the first Professor of Natural Science at the new University of Nebraska in Lincoln, serving from 1871 to 1883. We are able to present an assessment of Professor Aughey's contributions and to reassess his place in the history of the natural sciences in early Nebraska based on a clearer understanding of his published works and activities during his time at the university. In 1856, he received an ad endum degree from Pennsylvania College (now Gettysburg College). Two years later they conferred on him the more honorific degree of A. M. Aughey entered the Lutheran Theological Seminary at Gettysburg, Pennsylvania, in the fall of 1857 and was ordained in 1858 in the Evangelical Lutheran Church. After serving churches in Pennsylvania, he was called in 1864 to the congregation at the Emanuel Lutheran Church in Dakota City, Nebraska, where he resided until 1871 when he took the position at the University of Nebraska.

Aughey's career at the university was marked with successes and honors, but also criticism and questions about his basic knowledge of the sciences. While carrying a heavy teaching load at the university and the associated Latin school, Aughey volunteered his services to benefit the citizen of Nebraska, providing identifications of submitted plants, animals, rocks, soils, and minerals. He also did chemical analyses of soils, liquor, and the results of necropsies and autopsies, which led him to testify as an expert witness at several murder trials. He often presented public lectures around the state and worked for the Union Pacific Railroad conducting geological surveys in Wyoming and other points west. His extracurricular work, led Aughey to spend more and more time away from the university. Yet this work made it possible for him to start a natural history cabinet at the University of Nebraska, which evolved into the University of Nebraska State Museum.

Aughey's research subjects were expansive and included geology, paleontology, mineral resources, coal, entomology, flora, fauna, meteorology, geography, and soils. Although he produced some credible research, his tendency toward boosterism led him to promote some unscientific theories of the time. He espoused "rain follows the plow," a nineteenth-century theory of climatology. Yet his research was often more useful than not. He worked to help control the devastating swarms of migratory locusts and sought to discover and document the state's abundance of natural resources—coal, ground water, and native plants and animals. Because of his boosterism and perhaps too because he left the university after he was accused of forging the co-signatures on personal loans, historians and scientists have regarded Aughey as a fraud and have overlooked his scientific contributions to the state of Nebraska.

Even though Aughey was eventually cleared of the forgery charge, he resigned from the university and moved on to Wyoming where he became the Territorial Geologist. After initial successes in Wyoming in identifying petroleum resources, he became mired in yet another controversy. This time, he was accused of salting gold ore in several local mines, which led to his departure from the state in 1887. He passed the subsequent years of his life in Arkansas, Alabama, and Washington—always it seems, seeking to strike it rich. Aughey died on 3 February 1912 in Spokane, Washington.

ABSTRACT

In order to better evaluate Aughey's contributions to the natural history of Nebraska and the Great Plains, it is important to properly evaluate him in the tradition of the amateur American naturalist of the 1860s and 1870s. This was the tradition of the physician-naturalist, pastor-naturalist, and others who pursued natural history as a secondary avocation. Modern biology was emerging in the 1850s and was slowly replacing these generally-trained naturalists with experts who were college graduates from professionalized scientific disciplines. In fact, Aughey left the University of Nebraska in 1884 just as the field of natural sciences was professionalizing. He was replaced by Professor Lewis E. Hicks who had studied geology and zoology at Harvard University and was a student of Louis Agassiz.

As an amateur naturalist, Aughey was a "popularizer" of science. His original scientific contributions may be small, but he served the citizens of Nebraska by compiling, analyzing, and disseminating scientific information about the state. Botanist Charles Bessey, who succeeded Aughey's tenure, was able to recognize that the contributions made by Aughey were not insignificant, "Let us honor him for his scientific spirit which he maintained here in the day when science was small and weak, and which he carried to the end of his long life."

Keywords: abolitionism, agriculture, Alabama, amateur, Arkansas, artesian wells, coal, freshwater shells, gold, history of science, insect pests, migratory locust, minister, natural history, Nebraska, ornithology, petroleum, professional, professor, rainfall, surface geology, University of Nebraska, wild fruits, Washington, Wyoming

Fig. 1. Photograph of Samuel Aughey taken in 1871 as he was preparing to take up the position of Professor of Natural Sciences at the University of Nebraska. Courtesy of Erwin H. Barbour, Museum Photographs Series (RG 32-01-01). Archives & Special Collections, University of Nebraska–Lincoln Libraries.

Introduction

"Black hair, black eyes, full beard; smooth, round head; evenly-balanced brain, high forehead, intellectual predominant; height, five feet eleven inches; weight, one hundred and fifty pounds; sanguine, bilious temperament. He has naturally a warm, affectionate disposition; is pained at the sight of want or suffering, has more pity than censure for the wrong-doer, is full of love and meekness—emblematic qualities that adorn the coming Redeemer of the world"

(Edmunds 1871: 271-273).

A. C. Edmunds, Aughey's friend and first biographer, pens a vivid description of Samuel Aughey at age 39 and at the brink of making the most important career change of his life to become the first Professor of Natural Science at the new University of Nebraska in Lincoln. Over the next 12 years, Aughey would amass a record of staggering accomplishments, including many firsts, but his amateur scientific practices during an age of professionalization in science, as well as his questionable ethics, and controversial cultural views would garner him a group of detractors who persisted well into the latter half of the twentieth century. He was called a "charlatan" by Roscoe Pound, one of the leading jurists of the twentieth century (Manley 1967), and a "boomer" by Robert Manley, a prominent twentieth-century Nebraska historian (Manley 1967). But with each claim and controversy there are questions of accuracy that warrant investigation. For instance, Aughey left the University of Nebraska in 1883, after he was accused of forging signatures on personal loans. Amid the swirling controversy, the Regents asked for his resignation, only to withdraw their request after the accusations were judged to be false (Anonymous 1912, 1978).

In an attempt to resolve the enigma of Prof. Samuel Aughey, we have tried to document all claims and accomplishments made during his lifetime (Edmunds 1871, Andreas 1882, Bancroft Collection 1885) and those accomplishments attributed to him by others following his life (Anonymous 1912, 1978, Bessey 1912, Hayes, 1912, Kennedy 1977). With these new insights and a true understanding of Prof. Aughey's published works and activities, we are able to present a revised assessment of Prof. Aughey's contributions and to reassess his place in the history of the natural sciences in early Nebraska.

The obituary of Aughey in the University of Nebraska's alumni magazine by C. E. Bessey described him as a scientific pioneer. Most of the material in the obituary by Bessey was taken verbatim from a funeral address by the Rev. W. G. M. Hayes. Hayes' source of information was Aughey's only surviving child, Helen Aughey Fulmer. After reading Hayes' obituary one suspects that Mrs. Fulmer's account both romanticized and exaggerated her father's life and accomplishments (Aughey and Aughey-Fulmer 1918). Assembling information from different sources to verify Hayes' account presents a more complex and interesting picture of one of Nebraska's first resident scientists than that of a simple charlatan or pioneering scientist (Fig. 1).

The Early Years

Samuel Aughey, Jr., was the son of Samuel and Elizabeth Kepner Aughey. He and a twin sister, Elizabeth, were born on 8 February 1831, near Mifflin, Milford Township, Juniata County, Pennsylvania. His birth year was given as 1831 in Andreas (1882:1057), Bessey (1912:19), Hayes (1912), Aughey and Aughey-Fulmer (1918:220), Stover and Beachem (1932:37), and a family history (Gilbert et al. 1968); however, it was given as 1832 in Edmunds (1871: 271), a personal interview with Aughey in 1885 (Bancroft Collection 1885), and census records from 1900 (Alabama Census 1900). He was the third of 12 children and the eldest to live to adulthood (Gilbert et al. 1968). Young Samuel's childhood was described by Hayes in almost Lincolnesque terms as one of "toil and self-sacrifice," of "studying in bed by the light of tallow dips," and of ciphering out mathematical problems on fence rails at the end of the corn row. His childhood interest in natural history was expressed by making "large collections of fossils and Indian antiquities from his native valley."

A much less effusive portrait of Aughey's childhood appeared in a brief biography in *The Nebraska Farmer* while he was living in Lincoln (McBride 1878). It does give a picture of someone who labored on the family farm and enjoyed searching for natural history in the valley of Licking Creek where his home was located. In his youth, Aughey was said to be quiet and an "inveterate" reader of books. Among his favorite books were those on natural history subjects with "Goldsmith's Animated Nature" at the top of the list.

Aughey attended common school in the winter, probably at the Red Bank School House, and attended Tuscarosa Academy for six months (Gilbert et al. 1968). He taught school briefly in his home area before entering Pennsylvania College (now Gettysburg College) when he was 20. In 1856, "he received his *ad endum* degree, and two years later the degree of A. M. was conferred by his *alma mater*, for distinguished ability displayed in teaching" (Edmunds 1871:271). The A.M. degree was awarded by the college to almost all graduates who after three years showed "evidence of good moral character and progress in intellectual attainment. Aughey was awarded the degree by the Board of Trustees at their meeting of 27 April 1859" (David Hedrick personal communication).

After short term jobs teaching at the old Greensburg Academy and surveying, he entered the Lutheran Theological Seminary at Gettysburg, Pennsylvania, in the fall of 1857. In his personal life, Aughey married Elizabeth Catherine Welty in Hannastown, Westmoreland Co., Pennsylvania, a native of that place, on 14 October 1858 (Andreas 1882:1057-1058, Aughey and Aughey-Fulmer 1918, Stover and Beachem 1932:37, Gilbert et al. 1968). They had three children—Anna Acautha (born: 11 November 1859; died: 29 September 1863), Daniel Welty (b.: 23 March 1861; d.: 17 August 1861), and Helen Barbara (b.: 7 May 1867; d.: 21 July 1951). Helen, the only child to survive to adulthood, was born in Nebraska, and died in Pullman, Washington, where she was a long-time resident (Gilbert et al. 1968).

Samuel Aughey was ordained in 1858 and served at churches in Chester Springs, Chester County, Pennsylvania, in 1859, and then in Lionsville also in Chester County in 1860 (Swain personal communication). He had a passion for both theology and science, and was known for publicly sharing his opinions on controversial political issues, including his antislavery views, in the widely circulated pamphlet "The Renovation of Politics" (McBride 1878). This resulted in a division in his church, which finally led to his resignation" (Aughey and Aughey-Fulmer 1918: 221).

In Pennsylvania, Aughey worked at several other churches and as an army chaplain. However, church records do not indicate this military service and seem to account for his time during these years with two more churches (Swain, personal communication) in Blairsville, Indiana County, in 1862-1863 and Duncannon, Perry County, in 1863-1864. He left Pennsylvania for Nebraska where he arrived in Dakota City, Dakota County, in December 1864 as a "Home Missionary" and took charge of the First Lutheran Church and also organized the congregation in Ponca City, Dixon County (Aughey and Aughey-Fulmer 1918, Wolff 1950, Lund 1990).

Hayes (1912) painted a more dramatic picture of Aughey's activities during the Civil War, describing him as a secret agent for Abraham Lincoln who undertook a perilous government expedition to explore the lava flows of Idaho and Washington led by four Native American guides. There are neither records of his military service nor any record of this government expedition. The basis of these claims remains unclear.

Hayes (1912) inaccurately claimed that Aughey was the first white man to explore the Niobrara River and the first geologist to explore the Bad Lands. In fact, in 1849 (when Aughey was 17 years old, and still living at home), John Evans, working for David Dale Owen under the auspices of the Treasury Department, was the first geologist to explore the White River Bad Lands (then in the Territory of Nebraska, today in South Dakota). The expedition is well documented, and the fossil mammals that Evans collected, first described by the American paleontologist and naturalist Joseph Leidy, stirred enormous excitement in the scientific community (Owen 1852, Leidy 1853).

Hayes (1912) also included Aughey as a member of the 1859-1860 Hayden expedition that left St. Louis on 28 May 1859. The expedition under command of W. F. Raynolds, with F. V. Hayden as surgeon and naturalist, explored the drainages of the Yellowstone River in southeastern Montana and northeastern Wyoming, spending the winter layover at Deer Creek on the North Platte River in Wyoming. They returned to Nebraska, following the Missouri River to Fort Union, North Dakota, and then on to Omaha, Nebraska, where they disbanded on 4 October (Merrill 1924, Foster 1994). There is no mention of Aughey in any of the publications of Hayden covering this period of time, nor in the recent biography of Hayden. Aughey's account book, now at the Nebraska State Historical Society (RS3868AM), places him in Pennsylvania during the period of 1 July 1860 to 10 October 1861. There is no mention of Hayden or any exploration in 1860 in Aughey's biography in Andreas (1882:1057-1058). However, two newspaper articles in late 1880 place him ". . . in the west about a month in the company with Professor Hayden and other eminent geologists making a geological survey of portions of the Rocky Mountains" (*Nebraska State Journal*, 16 October 1880; *Lincoln Daily Globe*, p. 4, 11 November 1880). There are no known scientific publications from this expedition.

The Early Years in Nebraska—
1864 to 1871

Aughey's arrival in Dakota City in December 1864 until his move to the University of Nebraska in 1871 is poorly documented; nevertheless, enough information is available to outline his activities during this period. Aughey arrived in Dakota City as a "Home Missionary," serving the congregation at the Emanuel Lutheran Church and another in Ponca City. The church in Dakota City was the first Lutheran Church established in the Territory of Nebraska, organized in 1858 by the Rev. H. W. Kuhns. Rev. Aughey became the second pastor of the church, replacing Rev. Kuhns who moved to Omaha (Sailor 1958). During the years of his ministry Aughey used the parsonage, the house next to the church, as his home (Gilbert et al. 1968).

Several authors have stated that Aughey moved his family with him to Dakota City in December 1864 (Bolick 1993, Knoll 1995:14), but contemporary newspaper accounts curiously make little mention of his family. Although, the *Sioux City Journal* of 2 September, 1865, stated that "Rev. Samuel Aughey...has left for Pennsylvania and will return with his family in about six weeks" (*Sioux City Journal*, 1(51):3), it was not until 23 January 1866 that they published a brief mention of Aughey's arrival, "Rev. Samuel Aughey arrived here [Dakota County] last Friday [23 January 1866]." The paper never reported that the entire family had arrived in town; instead, there was mention of two sermons that he had given on the Sabbath (*Sioux City Journal*, 2(18):3).

The *Sioux City Journal* documented Aughey's religious and political activities in Dakota City: "Rev. Samuel Aughey held a communion meeting in the Lutheran church in this village on last Sabbath" (*Sioux City Journal*, 2(28):3), and "Rev. Samuel Aughey, of Dakota City, will deliver a temperance lecture at the Baptist Church [in Sioux City, IA], on Wednesday evening next, 17 April" (*Sioux City Journal*, 3(23):3). They also reported on the 4th of July suffrage speech that Aughey delivered in 1865, a short time after arriving in Dakota City: A few miles south of the city, Aughey declared to a group of citizens gathered under a grove of trees that "we must not withhold the ballot box from our negro soldiers" (*Sioux City Journal*, 1 (44):3).

In 1867, after nearly three years, Aughey resigned his pastorate "through failing health" to devote himself almost exclusively to scientific work (Knoll 1995). However, his first biographer A. C. Edmonds cites the year 1869, and provides a different occupation, stating that "Through failing health he resigned his pastoral work in 1869, and devoted his time to outside labor as a civil engineer" (Edmunds 1871:272). The exact nature of Aughey's failing health is unknown, but it is often provided, perhaps as an excuse, for other sudden changes in his life. At this time, given his outspoken support for temperance and the "Negro suffrage movement," and in particular, the right of African American Civil War soldiers to vote, it is possible that Aughey was quietly forced to resign.

Aughey's activities in the period from 1867 to 1871 were first documented by historian A. T. Andreas in 1882:

> Since 1867 he has been engaged exclusively in scientific work, was also engaged in making geological, miner-

alogical, botanical and conchological collections, in Dakota, Wyoming, and Nebraska, for scientific institutions, principally for Prof. Henry of the Smithsonian institute (Andreas 1882:1057).

Aughey's eulogists repeated Andreas's account, using similar language:

> ... we find him in 1867 devoting himself for the most part to scientific work and also engaging in making geological, mineralogical, botanical and conchological collections in Dakota, Nebraska, Colorado and Wyoming for scientific institutions, principally for Professor Henry of the Smithsonian Institution— indeed for 25 years thereafter he was an accredited representative of the Smithsonian Institution, to which he made regular reports (Hayes 1912; see also Bessey 1912, Aughey and Aughey-Fulmer 1918, Howard 1919, Knoll 1995).

However, an earlier biography in *The Nebraska Farmer* (McBride 1878) describes his natural history pursuits in northeastern Nebraska, but does not mention Joseph Henry or the Smithsonian Institution. Aughey may have embellished his own record—and then his early biographers simply repeated the information without fact checking.

Joseph Henry was Secretary of the Smithsonian Institution from 1846 until his death on 13 May 1878 (Rivinus and Youssef 1992). He opposed the idea "of collecting whatever animals, vegetables, and minerals struck the fancy of naturalists." He had developed his own interpretation of James Smithson's vaguely worded wishes, which he determined as calling for the development of entirely new knowledge and its diffusion to all of mankind. Secretary Henry only accepted newly appointed Assistant Secretary Spencer Fullerton Baird's private collection on the grounds that it included newly discovered American fauna and "that Baird's studies of the development of American vertebrates and their relationships provided new insights into science and natural history" (Rivinus and Youssef 1992: 64). Clearly, Henry was not inclined to accept small collections of specimens or artifacts from amateur naturalists. Aughey may have sent specimens for deposit in the U.S. National Museum collections, but Baird would have been his point of contact, not Henry.

In fact, Aughey was not listed in any of the reports to the Regents of the Smithsonian Institution as being one of its employees or contributors, nor is he listed among the numerous meteorological observers reporting data from across the United States to the Smithsonian and Henry (Schott 1872, 1876, 1881). A request to the Smithsonian Archives found no correspondence between Aughey and Henry. However, there are a few pieces of evidence that Aughey attempted to collaborate with the Smithsonian Institution. On 16 January 1876, he wrote to Ferdinand Vandeveer Hayden (Smithsonian Institution Archives, George P. Merrill Collection, RU 7177, Foder 21), but there is no letter from Hayden in response. The U. S. National Museum did record in the 1882 *Additions to the Collections of the Smithsonian Institution* four fossils collected by Aughey: *"Received*—Feb. 4; *Current Number*—11107; *Nature of Article*—4 Specs. Cretaceous & Laramie fossils; *Locality*—W. Nebraska; *Transportation Number*—[blank]; *Storage Number*—[blank]; *Received from*—Prof

Sam'l Aughey; *Address*—[blank]; *Acknowledged*—[check mark]; *Expenses*—[blank]" (Tammy L. Peters, Smithsonian Institution Archives, personal communication). And Secretary Baird's office sent a standard thank-you letter to Aughey for the fossil donation (Tammy L. Peters, Smithsonian Institution Archives, personal communication). But Baird, who had succeeded Henry, did not correspond directly with Aughey.

M. M. Warner's history of Dakota County, Nebraska, gives quite a different account of Aughey's activities during this period. According to Warner, Aughey was appointed as the County Superintendent of Public Instruction by County Commissioners on 3 December 1866, and replaced by them on 5 April 1869. He was again appointed by the County Commissioners to this position on 5 July 1869, in which he served until 12 October 1869 (Warner 1893:130). Aughey also was appointed as County Surveyor on 30 July 1869, by County Commissioners and he was elected to the position on 12 October 1869, which he held until replaced on 10 October 1871 (*Dakota City Mail*, 14 April 1871;Warner 1893:131).

At the time that he was the county surveyor in Dakota County, Aughey was speculating in land in nearby Wayne County (Stone 1952). In 1869 and 1870, he purchased 1920 acres using cash, military bounty scrip, and agricultural college scrip, making him one of the 35 largest individual landholders in the county. As Stone (1952) noted, those individuals who purchased over 1000 acres had plans other than farming the land because "Obviously no man, using the methods of farming then in practice, could farm all of such an area." Aughey held the land for only one year before reselling it in smaller units. Stone (1952) concluded that individuals who kept large holdings of land for less than 10 years were speculating in land "primarily interested in quick sale of the land for profits." Also, during Aughey's residence in Dakota City, he was engaged in real estate, with William Adair. This partnership was dissolved on 18 August 1871 as Aughey prepared to move to the University of Nebraska (*Dakota City Mail*, 1 September 1871).

The University Years—1871 to 1883

Hiring

The University of Nebraska was founded in 1869, but the first students did not matriculate until September of 1871. The primary requirement for the faculty of the new school was religious orthodoxy; all of the first professors had to be ordained ministers (Bolick 1993). The professorship of natural science was first offered to the Reverend Henry W. Kuhns, an ordained Lutheran minister, at a meeting of the Regents on 4 April 1871 (Watkins 1913: 294). Rev. Henry Welty Kuhns, D. D, was born in Greensburg, Westmoreland County, Pennsylvania, to John and Susan (Welty) Kuhns. He graduated from Pennsylvania College, Gettysburg, in 1856 and the Theological Seminary in Gettysburg in 1858. Rev. Kuhns went almost immediately to Nebraska following graduation, appointed by the Allegheny Lutheran synod as "the representative of the Evangelical Lutheran church to Nebraska and adjacent parts" (Morton 1906:517). Aughey probably knew Kuhns at Pennsylvania College and the Theological Seminary given that they both graduated in the same years. They also seem to have been related by marriage, as Aughey's wife was a Welty from Westmoreland County, Pennsylvania, and Kuhns brought Aughey to Nebraska as a missionary. At the Regent's meeting held 13 June 1871, Samuel Aughey was elected chair of natural sciences, after Mr. Kuhns declined to accept their previous offer (Watkins 1913:294). He instead recommended that they offer the position to Aughey. Aughey's letter of acceptance was dated 5 July 1871, and the Board of Regents recorded the letter on 5 September 1871. Aughey's appointment as the first Professor of Natural Sciences at the University of Nebraska was set to begin on 7 September 1871 (*Omaha Herald*, 15 June 1871, 24 August 1871; University of Nebraska Archives 1/1/1) (Figure 1).

Degrees

In commenting on Aughey's academic credentials Hayes (1912) stated: "On the occasion of a certain commencement season (1873) the degree of Ph.D. was conferred upon him simultaneously by the Pennsylvania College, Wittenberg College and the University of Ohio." Stover and Beachem (1932:37) and Wentz (1927:414-415) also give these institutions for Ph.D. degrees for Aughey, but with differing dates of conferment as follows: University of Ohio, 1874; Wittenberg College, 1875; Gettysburg College, 1876. In an early biography, McBride (1878) wrote that Aughey "received the honorary degree of Doctor of Philosophy from five different colleges and university," but he did not list them.

Records indicate that Aughey received a Ph.D. from Pennsylvania College (now Gettysburg College), but there is no evidence that Aughey received a Ph.D. from Ohio University in Athens, Ohio State University, or Miami University of Ohio (Goerler 1997 personal communication, McCabe 1997 personal communication, Schmidt 1997 personal communication). The *Alumni Record of Gettysburg College* (1832-1932), recorded that Aughey's doctoral degree was conferred in 1873. Peg Dalton, Archivist at Wittenberg College, Ohio, found no record of Aughey earning a higher degree at their institution (Dalton 1997 personal communication). In 1878, Aughey did, however, receive an LL.D. from Wittenberg College, which was associated with the Evangelical Lutheran Church (1927: 414-415 (Dalton 1997, Wentz, 1927: 414-415, and *Juniata Sentinel and Republican*, 31 July 1878).

Teaching

The teaching load at the fledgling University of Nebraska was extremely heavy by today's standards (Fig. 2); in the natural sciences, Aughey taught biology, geology, botany, chemistry, entomology and bee keeping, meteorology, mineralogy, ornithology, paleontology, physics, physiology, and zoology (Table 1). When called upon, he also filled in teaching responsibilities in other areas, such as German in the academic years 1871-72 and 1872-73, drawing and perspective drawing in 1875-76, and Latin classes on Virgil and Cicero in the 1877-78. Beginning in 1873-74 (except from 1880-81) Aughey also taught courses in the Latin School associated with the University, including physical geography and elementary courses in botany, chemistry, physics, and zoology (Table 1; Benton, 1872a, 1873, 1874a, 1875a, 1876; Fairfield, 1876, 1877, 1878, 1879, 1880, 1882; Hitchcock, 1883; Howard, 1919; UNL Archives 1/1/1—Box 2, Folder 26; Box 3, Folder 30; Box 4, Folders 38, 42, 46).

In an 1881 speech, Aughey (1881a) stated that he "taught six hours a day besides having the care of the chemical department and the founding of a museum." The class sizes of his courses can be seen in examples from 1877–1878 and 1881–1882, respectively: fall term—geology, 11 students; physical geography, 38; Virgil, 5; winter term—mineralogy, 4; Cicero, 18; ornithology, 7;

Fig. 2. Photograph of University Hall at the University of Nebraska. This was the first building constructed on campus where Aughey carried out all of his responsibilities for the University. Despite the building's substandard materials and poor construction, it was used until 1948. Courtesy of Erwin H. Barbour, Museum Photographs Series (RG 32-01-01). Archives & Special Collections, University of Nebraska–Lincoln Libraries.

spring term—zoology (senior) 4; elementary botany (first division), 25 and (second) 12; structural botany, 9; and first semester—biology, 29 students; physiology, 15; physical geography, 38; second semester—elementary botany, 33; structural botany, 9; zoology 18; paleontology, 2; mineralogy, 7; elementary zoology, 37 (University Archives 1/1/1, Box 2, f 26; 1/1/1, Box 4, f 42). Aughey claimed to have taught the following hours in the years listed above: fall term, 193 hours; winter term, 126; spring term, 182; first semester, 150; second semester, 261. Although the number of teaching hours are significant, he must have also spent many additional hours preparing for teaching and grading the resulting papers and examinations. According to Manley (1967) "Aughey quickly established himself as a popular teacher. Western students possessed an interest in science. More importantly, perhaps, Professor Aughey's courses proved to be 'snaps.'" We have not found other sources that claimed Aughey's teaching was below standard. In the *Hesperian Student*, the student newspaper, the comments on his teaching seem to be quite positive from early in his tenure. In an article in 1872, they wrote "Professor Aughey delivers a lecture to his class in Chemistry every morning at 9 o'clock. These lectures are very interesting, and are much more appreciated by the students than studying text books" (*Hesperian Student* 2(1): 3, 1872). Later in 1876, the they wrote "The class in Geology have been treated with some interesting discourses on Lithological Geology, since the return of Prof. Aughey" (*Hesperian Student* 5(10): 23, 1876). The content of some of these courses for agricultural students were briefly described in an early article in the *Nebraska City News* (13 June 1874).

Table 1. Courses taught by Samuel Aughey while employed at the University of Nebraska.

Courses Taught	Academic Years Courses Were Taught
University-level Courses	
Advanced Geology	1875-76
Agricultural Chemical Analysis	1872-73
Analytical Chemistry	1871-72, 1872-73, 1878-79
Bee Keeping	1879-80
Biology	1878-79, 1879-80, 1880-81, 1881-82, 1882-83
Botany	1871-72, 1872-73, 1873-74, 1874-75, 1876-77
Chemical Geology	1880-81, 1882-83
Chemistry Laboratory	1873-74, 1874-75
Cicero	1877-78
Drawing	1875-76
Entomology	1874-75, 1876-77, 1878-79
Geology	1871-72, 1872-73, 1873-74, 1875-76, 1876-77, 1877-78, 1878-79, 1879-80, 1880-81, 1882-83
Geology of Agriculture	1872-73
German	1871-72, 1872-73
Inorganic Chemistry	1872-73, 1873-74, 1874-75
Meteorology	1873-74, 1874-75, 1879-80, 1880-81, 1882-83
Mineralogy	1876-77, 1877-78, 1879-80, 1880-81, 1881-82, 1882-83
Organic Chemistry	1872-73, 1873-74, 1874-75
Ornithology	1877-78, 1879-80
Paleontology	1880-81, 1881-82, 1882-83

Table 1 (*continued*).

Courses Taught	*Academic Years Courses Were Taught*
Perspective Drawing	1875-76
Physics	1874-75, 1875-76
Physiology	1873-74, 1874-75, 1875-76, 1878-79, 1879-80, 1880-81, 1881-82, 1882-83
Physiology (Lectures to Classical Students)	1878-79, 1879-80
Structural Botany	1877-78, 1878-79, 1880-81, 1881-82, 1882-83
Virgil	1877-78
Zoology	1871-72, 1872-73, 1873-74, 1875-76, 1876-77, 1877-78, 1878-79, 1879-80, 1880-81, 1881-82, 1882-83
Zoology of Agriculture	1872-73

Latin School Courses

Elementary Botany (1st Division)	1877-78, 1878-79, 1879-80
Elementary Botany (2nd Division)	1875-76, 1877-78, 1878-79, 1879-80, 1881-82, 1882-83
Elementary Chemistry	1874-75
Elementary Physics (1st Division)	1879-80
Elementary Physics (2nd Division)	1873-74, 1874-75, 1879-80
Elementary Zoology	1881-82
Physical Geography	1873-74, 1874-75, 1875-76, 1876-77, 1877-78, 1878-79, 1881-82, 1882-83

However, the students began to complain about Professor Aughey's absences from campus. The earliest such article that we found in the student newspaper appeared in 1878:

> Prof. Aughey recently delivered a lecture in Des Moines on the 'Geology of Nebraska.' This is one of the Professor's best lectures and wherever delivered meets with encomiums from press and public. Why can't we have it delivered here? The subject is of interest to all students in general and to us in particular, and we doubt if a half a dozen of the students attending this term ever heard it (*Hesperian Student* 7(8): 477, 1878).

A similar complaint appeared in October 1879 (*Hesperian Student* 8(8): 185, 1879), as well as subsequent complaints about his absences, such as making a government survey in western Nebraska (*Hesperian Student* 9(11): 3, 1880), subpoenaed to Washington on scientific business (*Hesperian Student* 10(6): 4, 1881), and still in Washington with courses being taught by others "Editorials denouncing the manner in which these classes are taught are now in order" (*Hesperian Student* 10(8): 5, 1882). The latter article is followed by one on 1 February and another on 15 February, respectively, that continue this tone, "Won't Prof. Aughey be surprised when he gets back to find what funny changes have happened in the University! He will have a 'who's been here since I's been gone' sort of a look" (*Hesperian Student* 10(9): 4, 1882) and "Prof. Aughey was here three hours last week. He is not here now. He is in Omaha" (*Hesperian Student* 10(10): 4, 1882).

Aughey claimed that he was a proponent of the new idea of evolution by natural selection as proposed by Charles Darwin.

Fig. 3.--Photograph of the "Botanical Room" in University Hall at the University of Nebraska taken in 1884 at about the time of Aughey's departure from the University. Courtesy of Erwin H. Barbour, Museum Photographs Series (RG 32-01-01). Archives & Special Collections, University of Nebraska–Lincoln Libraries.

However, if Wilber's (1881a:2) review of one of Aughey's public lectures reflected his believes, they were quite far from those of Darwin:

> "Prof. Aughey quoted freely from the eminent scientists, Tyndall and Huxley, who have been considered as materialistic, and showed that their description of the absolute or first cause, presupposed an eternal, self-existent, unconditional mind. In short, the lecture was a splendid defense of modern science against the common suspicion of atheistic tendencies. It was the direct testimony of science for the recognition of the Supreme Ruler of the Universe."

Research

The most controversial aspect of Aughey's work during his tenure at the University was the quality of his research. Manley (1967) described Aughey's replies to queries from the public as "based upon a minimal amount of scientific investigation"; George E. Howard (1919), another historian of the University described Aughey as "a loveable personality" but continued that "the enormous burden laid upon his shoulders by the University did not tend to foster scientific precision." Lawrence Brunner, an internationally recognized expert on migratory locusts and one of the first students to study under Aughey at the University of Nebraska, used almost exactly the same language to assess his contributions: "His work was earnest and sincere, but with so much put upon him, scientific exactness could scarcely be expected" (Taylor 1931:181). This lack of precision was criticized by some of his botanical successors. Aughey had published a *Catalog of the Flora of Nebraska* in 1875. When H. J. Webber did a new catalog in 1890, he said "the first [Aughey's] was based, or appears to have been based, chiefly on range and distribution as given by authors, instead of specimens actually collected within the limits of the state and preserved for reference" (Webber 1890). Four years later, Roscoe Pound's criticisms were blunter, "subsequent researches have failed to confirm his estimates" of the species in the flora, and "his catalogue is substantially unreliable" (Pound 1894).

A recent search of the holdings of the botanical collections of the University of Nebraska State Museum document 164 sheets listing Aughey as the collector (Fig. 3). The majority of the collecting sites were in southeastern Nebraska in the vicinity of Lincoln, Lancaster County, with only two sheets from western Nebraska (Cheyenne Co. and Lincoln Co.), three sheets from the central part of the state (Fillmore Co.), and five sheets from the northeastern area (Dakota Co.). All collection dates were in 1873, 1874, or 1875. Even taking into account some attrition of specimens, this material does not appear to be sufficient to support a publication such as *Catalog of the Flora of Nebraska*.

Examination of Appendix 1 reveals that Aughey authored at least 77 publications. There may well be additional publications that we have not located because several mentioned by Bessey (1912), Hayes (1912), and Aughey and Aughey-Fulmer (1918) have not been found. Aughey's publications cover a wide range of topics, including agriculture, artesian wells, birds, flora, geology, horticulture, locusts, mollusks, petroleum, and physical geography.

Manley (1967) cited Aughey's involvement in the search for coal in Nebraska as another example of his boosterism and poor science. Yet this harsh critique doesn't take into account Aughey's good-faith encouragement of prospecting in the state, as coal beds were discovered in eastern Nebraska, even if later it was determined that they were not viable commercial beds. Aughey, ignoring F. V. Hayden's (1868, 1871) earlier conclusion that there were no workable coal beds in Nebraska, journeyed to the coalfield areas of Richardson County in April of 1873 (*Nebraska Advertiser*, 1 May 1873; *West Point Republican*, 8 May 1873) where he discovered coal beds and predicted that workable coal veins would be found in the Cretaceous or Tertiary deposits of the state. Manley writes in a disapproving tone that "Aughey had been telling the people of Nebraska that in all likelihood a gigantic deposit of coal lay under their state," and that "Spurred by Aughey's reports, and by a $4000 bounty offered by the state for the discovery of a twenty-inch vein of workable coal, eager prospectors scoured Nebraska for coal" (Manley 1967:113).

Manley does, however, acknowledge that although Aughey encouraged the search for usable coal deposits, when the data had accumulated, he concluded "correctly" that there were not usable deposits in Nebraska. And Manley notes that by 1880, Aughey "tried to convince settlers that the search for coal was in vain" (Manley 1967:114). Aughey's scientific field observations in the region are, more or less, sound applied science, and he was not the last university researcher to write about coal in Nebraska (Barbour 1908). Finally, it must be noted that the Honey Creek Coal Mine near Peru, Nemaha Co., contained a bed of coal that averaged 33 inches in thickness and ultimately yielded approximately 200,000 tons of coal (Barbour 1908, Genoways 1989).

Aughey made time for more research based scientific pursuits while in Nebraska, but the level of his involvement and official roles were often exaggerated by Aughey and may have misled historians like Manley who attempted to write accurate biographies. Bessey (1912), Hayes (1912), and Aughey and Aughey-Fulmer (1918) all stated that Aughey was a member of U. S. Entomological Commission in 1877 and Aughey himself claimed in an 1885 interview that he "Was apptd in 1875 a commissioner of U. S. Entomologist" (Bancroft Collection, 1885). The United States Entomological Commission was created by an act of Congress on 3 March 1877 to investigate and report upon the depredations of the Rocky Mountain grasshopper in the West. The three most learned economic entomologists in the United States were appointed to form the Commission: Charles V. Riley, the organizer of economic entomology in this country, then serving as State Entomologist of Missouri; Alpeus S. Packard, Jr., one of the greatest American entomologists and at the time director of the Peabody Academy of Science and chief editor of the *American Naturalist*; and Cyrus Thomas, one of the foremost early economic entomologists of America, and then serving as State Entomologist of Illinois (Swenk 1937:37, Foster 1994:275–276). Samuel Aughey was not a member of this Commission. However, during a visit by Thomas to Minnesota, northwestern Iowa, and Nebraska "Prof. Samuel Aughey, of the State University at Lincoln, was engaged as assistant for that portion of the district" (Riley 1878b:10-11). In Appendix XXVI of Riley's (1878b: [270]) first annual report for the Entomological Commission "Aughey, Prof. Samuel, Lincoln, Lancaster County" is listed under Nebraska in the "List of Correspondents." Elsewhere in this same publication, a section is identified as "Being a journal kept by Prof. Samuel Aughey, of the University of Nebraska, as Special Assistant of the Commission."

Manley (1967) is critical that Aughey did not act quickly to investigate the Rocky Mountain locust plagues, arguing that this was the result of his wanting "to do nothing to damage the state's 'prospects,'" and that "Perhaps this is why Professor Aughey had little to say about the problem in 1874 and 1875, the worst years of the plague" (Manley 1967: 114). However, Aughey's activities studying the grasshoppers in 1875 were recorded in Nebraska newspapers (*Falls City Journal*, 24 June 1875; *Nebraska State Journal*, p. 2, 4, 25 June 1875; *Nebraska Advertiser*, 1 July 1875), and as one of the newspapers noted, the legislature in the last session had failed to appropriate funds for more extensive work on the problem (*Nebraska State Journal*, 3 September 1875). In addition, on 1 January 1877, Aughey published recommendations for controlling insects (Aughey 1877a), and, as noted, the federal government did not get the U. S. Entomological Commission organized until 1877. Aughey did, in fact, play a role in the commission's investigation of the Rocky Mountain locust problem, supplying his field observations that he had made over a several year period while assisting Professor Thomas during his field work in Nebraska (*Nebraska State Journal*, 15 June 1877).

Aughey did, however, engage in questionable science, as he was one of the leading proponents of the "rain follows the plow," and argued that "It is the great increase in absorptive power of soil, wrought by cultivation, that has caused, and continues to cause an increasing rainfall in the State" (Aughey

1880a:44). His work on this theory has brought more criticism of his scientific abilities than any of his other ideas. Even in recent years, Knoll (1995: photograph 6) in his history of the University of Nebraska-Lincoln, wrote that Aughey "was a great proselytizer of the theory that 'rain follows the plow'; perhaps he invented the theory." According to Knoll (1995:14-15), Aughey's "speeches and publications boosting the trans-Missouri West as suited for agriculture were reprinted by the railroads to encourage settlement in the Great American Desert. His explanation for this increase in rainfall is ingenious. As the land is broken, he said the absorptive power of the soil is increased and the land becomes 'like a huge sponge. The soil gives this absorbed moisture slowly back to the atmosphere by evaporation. Thus year by year as cultivation of the soil is extended, more of the rain that falls is retained to be given off by evaporation or to produce springs.'" Manley (1967; see also Kollmorgen 1935) expressed a similar view, Aughey "described the unmistakable increase in rainfall, which must have allayed some apprehensions; and he made every effort to publicize other aspects of Nebraska's physical endowment—especially the wondrous quality of Nebraska's soils."

If we consider that meteorological science at this time was nescient, Aughey's support of this theory seems more misguided than overtly bad scientific practice. The theory that rainfall follows the plow was not "invented" by Aughey, it instead was proposed by Josiah Gregg in his book *Commerce of the Prairies,* published in 1844 (Kollmorgen 1935). The theory was finally discredited, but not until the 1890s, and today seems foolish to those of us considering it today (Foster 1994:182). After first mentioning the idea of rain following the plow in a report for F. V. Hayden's U. S. Geological and Geographical Survey of the Territories, Cyrus Thomas referred to it four years later—more critically—in the course of another lengthy report for Hayden on the agriculture of the West. Hayden, as director of the survey, called attention to the popularity of the theory twice more without giving it an endorsement or trying to discredit it. However, he did publish the supportive reports from two other writers, R. S. Elliott, working in Kansas, and Samuel Aughey, in the results of his survey (Foster 1994:182-183; correspondence Aughey to Hayden, Smithsonian Archives, 11 November 1875).

What critics of Aughey within Nebraska have forgotten is that he was not the only scientist who espoused a climatic theory that was later discredited (for brief review of some of these ideas see Pound 1946, Swanberg 2019). In fact, Libecap and Hansen (2002) writing in the early twenty-first century stated about "rain follows the plow" and similar meteorological theories, stated that when they are "placed into the context of the limited climate and agricultural information at hand, they are understandable as responses to observed conditions." It must be remembered that as settlement of Nebraska began in the 1850s through the 1880s that rainfall was increasing and only with the occurrence of droughts in the 1890s could this wet period be seen as a climatic fluctuation, rather than a permanent weather change (Smith 1947, Libecap and Hansen 2002). There was far less coverage of the rainfall issue in the Nebraska newspapers than other controversies in which Aughey was involved, because residents understood that the rainfall was increasing (*Red Cloud Chief*, 26 February 1880).

More questionable in terms of scientific practice is Aughey's report on the efficacy of birds in reducing the plagues of Rocky

Mountain locusts. One begins to wonder about his standards as a scientist when reading his report of hummingbirds eating the "locusts." It was these studies that formed the basis of Andreas' (1882:1057) claim made while Aughey was still living in Nebraska, "He was the first man in the United States who ever determined the exact food of the various birds." Mrs. H. J. Taylor writing for the *Wilson Bulletin* in 1931 listed Aughey as one of two "forerunners" of economic ornithology. The author is complimentary of Aughey's work, especially his early calls for the conservation of birds to control insects (Taylor 1931).

Ellet Hoke (2000, 2005, 2011) presented a very enlightening analysis of Aughey's work on the "Catalogue of the land and fresh-water shells of Nebraska," published in 1877. Not only does Hoke's work give important insights into Aughey's work on this particular group of animals, but also it provides deeper insights into his work as a scientist. Hoke (2000) concluded that the existing specimens in the University of Nebraska State Museum are not sufficient to support Aughey's work, but there are enough original catalogue entries to evaluate his publication. Of the 83 species of mollusks reported by Aughey from Nebraska, 58 represent currently recognized taxa. Nineteen of the 58 modern taxa are represented by specimens in the museum's collection, but at least some of them may have been taken outside of Nebraska. Hoke (2000) concluded that at least 16 or 28% of the 58 modern taxa were definitely in error because they have not been taken elsewhere in the Missouri River Basin. "Of the seven specimens surviving with names that appeared in Aughey's paper, only two are correctly identified," which is a 71% error rate.

Although these are only rough estimates of the errors present in the mollusk publication, they do raise serious questions about Aughey's ability to identify these animals. Hoke (2000) believed that these misidentifications could have had several potential sources. He raises two important issues that may have affected Aughey's ability to accurately identify species: Aughey may have lacked the appropriate library materials for making the identifications, and the synoptic material may have not been identified properly. Hoke found some evidence of the latter problem in the existing collection materials, making the point that "Many mollusks are difficult to identify due to the wide range of variation in the shells," consequently considerable time and study are necessary to identify these materials. (As we have documented, time was not one of the things that Professor Aughey enjoyed at the University of Nebraska.) Hoke (2011:11) in his most recent publication presented an updating of the Unioniod records presented by Aughey (1877) to help correct the historic record, but he concluded that "all information given by Aughey is suspect."

John Wesley Powell (1878, 1879) in 1878 made a proposal to change the existing system for disposition of the Public Domain in the arid lands west of the 100th parallel under the Homestead Act, Timber Culture Act, and Desert Land Act. Powell recognized that irrigation would be necessary in this area and proposed that one of two types of land grants be made—no more than 80 irrigated acres be granted along with a small area of pasturage land or 2560 acres of pasturage land be granted but it must include small tracts of irrigated lands. Powell's proposal caused a great outcry in the West because it was misinterpreted, either intentionally or unintentionally, to be a call for the closing of the Public Domain in this vast area (Worster 2001). Aughey with C. D. Wilber (1880) authored the Nebraska response to Powell's proposal, which was submitted to Robert W. Furnas, President of the Nebraska State Horticultural Society, and Martin Dunham, President of the State Agricultural Society. Their arguments were based around two points—the soils of the West were chemically equal to any on the American continent and that rainfall was increasing from East to West, which, as we have seen, it was doing in 1880 (Manley 1967:111-112). Congress did not accept Powell's ideas because of the political pressure from the West. When the drought cycle returned to these areas in the 1890s major irrigation projects became necessary and farming is still only possible in this region with irrigation.

Bessey (1912), Hayes (1912), and Aughey and Aughey-Fulmer (1918) all stated that Aughey was a member of U. S. Artesian Well Commission in 1881 and Aughey asserted in an 1885 interview that he "Was also apptd U. S. Artesian Well Comm., apptd 1880." (Bancroft Collection 1885). Aughey was listed as one of the Artesian Well Commissioners appointed by George B. Loring, Commissioner of Agriculture, Department of Agriculture, along with C. A. White, Smithsonian Institution, and Horace Beach (White et al. 1882). The purpose of this Commission was to examine the plains east of the Rocky Mountains to determine where water could be obtained for the purposes of irrigation (Andreas 1882:1058). The Commission's report was published in 1882 (White et al. 1882).

In Aughey's (1880a) *Sketches of the physical geography and geology of Nebraska*, he mentions the discovery of human artifacts in close association with fossil elephantine bones (one site in northwestern Iowa and one near Omaha) buried deep in loess deposits. This was not the first, but it was an early, potential documentation of the contemporary occurrence between mammoths and humans. The implications of this observation for the age of humans in North America was certainly recognized by authors trying to answer this question, which is still being studied today (McGee 1889).

Both Bessey (1912) and Hayes (1912) state that Aughey had publications that included "Material Resources of Nebraska, 1877," "History of Nebraska, 1878," and "Genesis of the Rocky Mountains, 1882." These publications are not mentioned in Andreas (1882: 1057-1058) and the Bancroft interview only states "also wrote a history of Nebraska" (Bancroft Collection 1885). We have not found publications by Aughey with these titles. He did author two chapters on surface geology and wild fruit in a book authored by E. A. Curley in 1876 entitled *Nebraska; its advantages, resources, and drawbacks*, and he wrote a chapter on economic and superficial geology of Nebraska for a book by L. D. Burch in 1878, entitled *Nebraska as it is: resources, advantages and drawbacks, of the Great Prairie State.* These are as close as we can match a title concerning the "Material Resources of Nebraska." Aughey wrote chapters on "Geology" and "Physical and Natural Features" for a book by A. T. Andreas in 1882, entitled *History of the state of Nebraska.* But we have not been able to find any publication that has anything to do with the origin of the Rocky Mountains, but we can't rule out the possibility that one exists, especially as a chapter in a longer book.

McBride wrote in his 1878 biography that "Some of his scientific papers have been translated and published in the principal European scientific journals." Yet we found no evidence of such publications. Another interesting statement that McBride (1878) made is that "During his younger years Prof. Aughey wrote under a 'nom de plume,' but since connection with the University he has invariably written under his own signature." We can't verify or deny this claim, but "Renovation of Politics" written in 1860 was published under his signature.

Service

About 65 years after Aughey's death, President of the University of Nebraska Ronald Roskens wrote that his "spirit is still felt" at the University. And he "set the standards of public service which through the years have been magnified and enhanced by faculty members of this institution" (Kennedy 1977). Indeed, Aughey was not only assigned a heavy teaching load, but he was answering scientific inquiries that were being submitted from around the state. As late as 1882, Professor Aughey still was receiving the accolades of students: "The professor of Natural Science is usually in his room from early in the morning until after eleven at night, and many of the other professors work equally as hard" (*Hesperian Student* 11(4):2, 1882). Part of what was keeping him in the laboratory was almost every sort of chemical analysis: soil, clay, shale, well water, coal, lignite, sugar beets, corn, patent medicines ("quantitative analysis of Mrs. Winslow's soothing syrup for Dr. Hurlbut, Lincoln"), and liquor ("quantitative analysis of thirteen varieties of liquor from Lincoln for Lincoln Temperance Society," and "of old Bourbon for James Sullivan"). He also performed autopsies and necropsies: "quantitative analysis of the stomach of Mrs. Burnham for the Cass County Commissioners," and "quantitative analysis of the stomach of a poisoned horse" (Anonymous 1874, *Hesperian Student* 3(6):5, May 1874, Bolick 1993).

41

Aughey also was involved with chemical analyses in murder cases by poisoning. In fact, it was his activities in testifying at murder trials that lead to some early criticism of his work and questioning of his expertise. Aughey testified for the prosecution in Grand Island in the case of Frank Lawrence who was accused of poisoning his father with prussic acid. Lawrence was acquitted when Aughey's analyses were questioned and criticized by two experts from Chicago brought in by the defense (*The Independent*, 10 June 1880). This resulted in comments in the newspapers, "Prof. Aughey had better look up his chemical analysis before he hires out as an expert" (*Omaha Daily Bee*, p. 2, 2 June 1880) and "To accuse Aughey of ignorance and bungling in a matter where life and death were at stake, cannot be overlooked by him, nor by the people" (*Weekly State Democrat*, p. 2, 11 June 1880). Fortunately for Aughey, in another case that quickly followed, this time involving arsenic poisoning, the defendant was convicted based on his testimony, quieting the criticism for a while (*Nebraska State Journal*, 15 June 1880).

One of Aughey's problems was that many of his service duties often took him away from Lincoln. Some of these travels can be documented from his reports to the University including those he undertook in 1874-75 (Aughey 1875c:27-30):

> I made exploring journeys into far up the Republican Valley, to the region around Kearney and Lowell, to the northern, eastern, and south-eastern part of the State, to North Platte, Sydney, and to Pine Bluffs [Wyoming], on the Union Pacific Railroad, and to many other points. I have traveled over three thousand

Fig. 4.--Photograph of the Museum or Cabinet in University Hall at the University of Nebraska taken in 1884 at about the time of Aughey's departure from the University. Courtesy of Erwin H. Barbour, Museum Photographs Series (RG 32-01-01). Archives & Special Collections, University of Nebraska–Lincoln Libraries.

miles in these expeditions in Nebraska alone; but with one exception, all these long journeys have been made during vacation.

The following year, he wrote "I made one trip of exploration to the western boundary of the State, two to the Nemaha river, three to the Blue rivers, and to many points on the various railroad lines in Nebraska. Most of these journeys, which extended over three thousand (3,000) miles, were performed in vacation" (Aughey 1876e:14, 17).

Aughey's travels in 1877, while making investigations for the U. S. Entomological Commission, included the following documented visits to counties in Nebraska: *March*—Buffalo, Kearney, Phelps, Harlan, Furnas, Red Willow, Hitchcock; *April*—Hitchcock, Dundy, Lancaster, Douglas; *May*—Lancaster; *June*—Lancaster, Johnson, Richardson, Clay, Dodge, Nemaha, Buffalo, Saline, Lincoln; *July*—Keith, Buffalo, Colfax, Douglas, Lancaster, Cass, Woodbury [Iowa], Dakota, Dixon; *August*—Dakota, Yankton [South Dakota], Knox, Douglas, Lancaster. Almost certainly some of this travel and preparation of reports was done at time other than vacation, but given the importance of controlling migratory locusts to the future of the state, this probably had official sanction. Aughey's report on "Work outside of the University" (UNL Archives, 1/1/1, Box 2, F. 26) for year ending 12 June 1878 states:

> For the purpose of fostering an interest in science and the work of the University, and of making scientific collections for the cabinet I have accepted twenty four invitations to lecture in various parts of the State during the last year. I have also gone to various points

44

to make geological determinations and to collect specimens. Great numbers of objects in natural history are
sent to me to determine and classify, or to identify,
and this often requires a great deal of time.

Although Aughey clearly performed considerable service for
the University and the people of Nebraska, it also is clear from
some of his reports that this work did not come without a price
and some personal aggravation, as Aughey made clear in his
report to the Chancellor in 1876, "The most onerous work of
this department continues to be the constant assistance that is
asked for by the public for identifying rocks, fossils, plants, etc.,
and in conducting the extensive correspondence which results
from the nature of such a position in a new state" (Aughey
1876e:14, 17).

Administration

Aughey also conducted administrative work for the University,
serving two terms as the Dean of College of Literature, Science
and Arts in 1874-1875 and 1879-1881. Aughey also served as the
Curator of the Cabinet and Herbarium (Fig. 4), being officially
appointed by the Board of Regents on 24 June 1874; although
it is clear from the records that he filled this position from the
beginning of his association with the University. He continued
to serve in this capacity until the end of his tenure at the University (Benton 1872b, 1873, 1874b, 1875b, Fairfield 1876, 1877,
1878, 1879, 1880, 1882, Hitchcock 1883, Watkins 1913, *Nebraska
State Journal* 24 June 1874). In 1874, a brief article in the *Kearney Junction Times* (p. 3, 29 January 1874), provides a fascinating

glimpse of the cabinet and herbarium, "here are many geological specimens from different parts of the State and of the West. There are near a thousand rejected models from the Patent Office at Washington" and "The Herbarium proved of great interest. In this Prof. Aughey is keeping a specimen of every plant to be found in the State." Just over a year later, the *Nebraska City News* (p. 2, 27 February 1875) describes the growth of the cabinet and museum under Aughey's leadership, "but the museum room seemed to be of particular interest to the rural observers, the cabinet and museum containing some eight thousand specimens. The Herbarium is furnished with more than seven hundred different species of plants of this State. Prof. Aughey has some 60 species of moths and 3,500 specimens of bugs."

Twice during his tenure at the university, Aughey was mentioned as a potential candidate to be chancellor. When Chancellor Benton resigned in 1876, some of the state newspapers, such as the *Daily Nebraska Press* wrote "Many of our more prominent and influential citizens advocate Prof. Samuel Aughey for the position" (p. 2, 25 March 1876). However, the Board of Regents selected Edmund B. Fairfield, a minister, former President of Hillsdale College, and the 12th Lt. Governor of Michigan, to fill the position. As the relationship between Fairfield and the Regents became strained in early 1880, Aughey's name again was mentioned in newspapers around the state regarding the position, and were both pro (*Omaha Evening Bee*, 5 January 1880) and con (*The Enterprise*, 7 January 1880). Fairfield was not replaced until two years later.

Honors and Recognition

A measure of a person's professional stature is the honors and recognition that one receives during their lifetime. Professor Samuel Aughey certainly received enough recognition during his years in Nebraska to believe that his professional colleagues respected him at the time. He delivered the Nebraska address at the U. S. Centennial in Philadelphia, Pennsylvania, in 1876 (Bancroft Collection 1885, Bessey 1912, Hayes 1912, Aughey and Aughey-Fulmer 1918, Diffendal 1976). Aughey delivered this address (1876f) on the geology, topography, soil, natural history, and weather of Nebraska in Judges' Hall on 26 October, one of twenty-seven speeches given by representatives of various state and territories (Diffendal 1976).

Professor Aughey was the first President of the Nebraska Academy of Science (Nebraska Academy of Sciences 1880a, 1880b, Bessey 1912, Hayes 1912, Aughey and Aughey-Fulmer 1918, UNL Archives 50/0/0) and was re-elected each year though 1884 (Schultz 1982, 1986). The Academy was organized on 29 and 30 January 1880, in Omaha, with major support from the Union Pacific Railroad. Aughey's election certainly confirmed that his contemporaries placed him as a leader of science in Nebraska, and under his direction, membership grew to 75 Charter Members from 18 communities across the state. But within a year, Aughey was criticized in the pages of the *Omaha Daily Bee* by E. Rosewater, editor of the *Bee,* who suggested that rather than calling the organization an academy of sciences: "Why not call it the Nebraska Debating Society or the 'Aughey and Wilber club for the promotion of geological surveys'" (*Omaha Daily Bee,* p. 2, 17 January 1881).

As early as 1872, Aughey was elected to the Board of Directors of the Lincoln Hospital Board, with the mission of establishing a hospital in the city (*Nebraska State Journal*, 8 June 1872). Aughey attended the organizational meeting of Nebraska State Historical Society held in Lincoln 25 September 1878 and was requested to serve on the Constitution and By-Laws Committee (Furnas 1885:14-15). The following day he presented the report for the Committee on Constitution and By-Laws, which was adopted. In the election held under these new rules, he was elected the first Recording Secretary of the Society (Furnas 1885:15-16, Diffendal 1978). On 23 January 1879 and 20 January 1880, he was re-elected Recording Secretary for the Nebraska State Historical Society (Furnas 1885:16-17, Diffendal 1978). In 1880, Aughey was appointed to a committee to secure the cooperation of County Historical and Old Settlers' Association. On 11 January 1881 and 17 January 1883, he was again re-elected to the position of Recording Secretary after having served through 1882, because there was no annual meeting during the year (Furnas 1885:21). In 1883, Aughey was appointed to a resolutions committee (Furnas 1885:21).

Prof. Aughey was an early and active member of Nebraska State Horticulture Society, serving as a Committee of One on Entomology in relations to Horticulture for several years and then latter as the Essayist for Entomology and Geology (Furnas 1877:21, 1879:6, 1885, Allan 1885:4). On 17 January 1878 Prof. Aughey was "elected honorary life member...of the Nebraska State Horticultural Society in recognition of his...valuable services for years in furnishing essays on various subjects, statistics, and other information to this society" (Furnas 1879: 28).

On 30 March through 1 April in 1880, the Nebraska State Teachers' Association held their fourteenth annual meeting in Seward. Aughey presented the opening lecture on the final day of the meeting entitled "The Geology of Seward County." Later in the day, Professor Aughey was elected president of the association for the next year (*Omaha Evening Bee*, 5 April 1880; *Blue Valley Blade*, 8 April 1880).

Several authors (Andreas 1882:1058, Bessey 1912:19, Hayes 1912; Aughey and Aughey-Fulmer 1918) claimed membership for Aughey in several regional and national professional societies, including the St. Louis Academy of Sciences, Iowa Academy of Sciences, Buffalo Academy of Science, and American Academy for the Advancement of Sciences. We have only been able to confirm his membership in the St. Louis Academy of Science and the Iowa Academy of Sciences. On 15 May 1876, Charles V. Riley, President of the St. Louis Academy of Science, following a discussion led by Judge Nathaniel Holmes concerning "Man and the Elephant in Nebraska" based upon Aughey's report published in the Hayden Survey proposed Dr. Samuel Aughey for corresponding membership in the Academy. On 5 June 1876 with President Riley again presiding, stated that "Dr. S. Aughey, Lincoln, Neb." was elected a Corresponding Member. A letter from Dr. Samuel Aughey, acknowledging his election as a Corresponding Member, was read at the 19 June 1876 meeting (Riley 1878a:ccxii-ccxviii). Aughey was the 171st Corresponding Member elected to the St. Louis Academy of Science since its founding in 1856 (Nipher 1886:viii-xii).

None of the information available from the Iowa Academy of Sciences supports the claim that Aughey was a member of the

Iowa Academy; however, a brief article in the *Des Moines Register* (19 February 1879, p. 3) stated that "Prof. Samuel Aughey, Ph.D. of the University of Nebraska, was duly elected a corresponding member." From 1875 to 1880 membership in the Iowa academy was limited to 30 Fellows and Aughey was only a corresponding member (Bessey 1880). No data for the Iowa Academy of Science seem to be available for the years 1881-1887, but it was reformed in 1887, without Aughey being listed as a member (Call 1892, Ross 1918). We have not found conclusive evidence of Aughey's memberships in the Buffalo Academy of Science and American Academy for the Advancement of Sciences.

"He held the then honorary position of State Geologist of Nebraska," was claimed for Aughey by both Bessey (1912) and Hayes (1912). However, according to Merrill (1920:290-291):

> Prior to 1901 no geological surveys of Nebraska had been undertaken under direct appropriations from the legislature, although an attempt was made in 1877 to get a bill through the State Legislature to complete the work as left by the United States geologist, F. V. Hayden. Samuel Aughey, of the State University, would appear to have been actively interested and at one time aspired to the directorship.

There does not seem to be any evidence that Prof. Aughey ever received an official honorary appointment as the State Geologist for the State of Nebraska, but given his publications on the geology of the state such a designation would have been appropriate.

At the zenith of Professor Aughey's tenure at the University, he was selected to deliver the main address at the tenth anniversary of the founding of the University. His charter day address "The Ideas and the Men that Created the University of Nebraska" was delivered on 15 February 1881. It was a modest recounting of the early history of the University with an emphasis on the faculty and first chancellor.

Non-university Activities

During the years that he served as a professor, Aughey, according to Hayes (1912), remained active in the ministry, having "organized a Lutheran church some 12 miles from Lincoln and was its regular pastor for eight to 10 years." This fact is supported by Andreas (1882:1086) who stated that Professor Aughey and the Rev. Kuhlmann, a missionary pastor, formed the Trinity Evangelical Lutheran Church in Waverly, Lancaster Co. According to Andreas (1882:1086), Aughey held services there for a number of years until a regular pastor was engaged in July 1880.

Departure from University

As the years passed, there was growing unhappiness with Aughey in many quarters of the state and university. Edward Rosewater, founder and editor of the *Omaha Daily Bee*, was the first to use the word "charlatan" to described Aughey's research (*Omaha Evening Bee*, 5 December 1878) and was heavily critical of his time away from the university giving public lectures. Rosewater continued his campaign against Aughey until he left the university, arguing that if Aughey wished to continue advertising himself, he should "join Barnum in the unrivalled show business" (*Omaha Daily Bee*, p. 2, 15 May 1880). Rosewater's comments always included questions about Aughey's time away from the university. When the Regents fired three professors Rosewater queried, "Why do the regents retain Professor Aughey, who is absent from his post of duty most of the time?" (*Omaha Daily Bee*, p. 4, 30 January 1882). Finally, Rosewater accused Aughey of "abusing his title as a professional endorser of patent medicines and bogus inventions" (*Omaha Daily Bee*, p. 4, 11 July 1883). His questionable endorsements included a cure for rheumatism, a cure for hog cholera (*Nebraska Advertiser*, 4 November 1880), a Colorado paving stone (*Omaha Daily Bee*, 9 July 1883), and novelty stone (*Columbus Era*, 11 May 1878).

After about ten years, the Board of Regents became well aware of these disparagements, especially of concern to them was the amount of time that Aughey spent in Wyoming, investigating coal and oil resources, which made them question whether he had financial interests in these fields. The precipitating factor in causing a break between Aughey and the University seems to have been a financial scandal involving "forged endorsements" in 1883 (Anonymous 1978, Knoll 1995). Lancaster County court records show four judgments against Aughey that summer—The First National Bank of Lincoln vs. Samuel Aughey and T. M. Marquette (appearance 3604, 26 July 1883); The First National Bank of Lincoln vs. Samuel Aughey and W. H. B. Stout (appearance 3605, 26 July 1883); Frank L. Sheldon vs. Samuel Aughey (appearance 3606, 26 July 1883); John P. Dorr vs. Samuel Aughey (appearance 3607, 27 July 1883). Sheldon's case was dismissed upon request of his attorney on 14 August 1883, and the remaining three were dismissed upon request of the plaintiffs' attorneys on 29 October 1883. In each case, the court judged that the defendants could recover their costs from the plaintiffs (Nebraska State Historical Society Archives, Lancaster County District Court, Appearance Docket "L" and Journal "I").

These cases involved signature loans that Aughey had obtained in the amount of about $5000 that were endorsed by prominent Lincoln business men (*Lincoln Journal Star*, 28 July 1883). Aughey claimed that the endorsements had been gathered for him by a man who owed him a great deal of money, D. C. Vigenham, but Aughey did not know where Vigenham was or even if that was his real name. Aughey did produce a letter from Vigenham, taking full responsibility for the forgeries on the loans. However, the letter from Vigenham was so poorly written and the forgeries were so skillfully prepared that authorities did not believe that same person had produced them (*Omaha Daily Bee*, 28 July 1883). In a letter to A. A. Childs, dated August of 1883 (Nebraska State Historical Society Archives, RG3868AM), Aughey wrote "I can assure you before God that I am innocent of the charge of forgery—innocent as an angel." He continued, "My enemies, especially those who have denounced me for being an evolutionist and a heretic, are making the most out of it." Aughey was able to arrange loans from friends and supporters to repay the forged loans thus avoiding legal action and causing the dropping of the lawsuits (*Fremont Weekly Herald*, 16 August 1883; *Nebraska State Journal*, 25 August 1883),

On 15 August 1883 at a meeting of the Board of Regents, a report prepared by William J. Armstrong was submitted on Aughey's behalf, presenting his defense against the charges of forgery. Aughey offered to resign at a future date to save the University from adverse publicity but he requested "a leave of absence until that time in order to prepare his complete vindication" (Armstrong 1883:2; *Nebraska State Journal*, 18 August 1883). Aughey subsequently met with the Board of Regents on 9 November 1883, presenting them the additional evidence requested particularly as to the existence of the man D. C. Vigenham. After examining the evidence, the Regents "passed a resolution declaring their belief in Professor Aughey's innocence and declining to accept his resignation...tendered in August last" (*Nebraska State Journal*, p. 3, 10 November 1883). Aughey thanked the Board members for their thorough examination of the evidence but re-tendered his resignation from the university effective immediately (*Nebraska State Journal*, 10 November 1883; *Omaha Daily Bee*, 21 November 1883). Accounts in the student newspaper gave his reasons for the departure as "his failing health" (*Hesperian Student* 12(4):3, 15 November 1883). Local newspapers stated that he had "engagements for scientific work in the west" (*Nebraska State Journal*, p. 3, 10 November 1883). The magnitude of the scandal can be judged by events 36 years later. In May 1919, Aughey's daughter, Helen, wrote the current chancellor of the University, Samuel Avery, offering to endow a scholarship in her father's name. Avery refused the money, writing "I am inclined to think that under the circumstances perhaps you would prefer to have the memorial in some other institution where there is no forgotten record that might possibly be brought to light" (University of Nebraska Archives 2/9/1).

The Wyoming Years—1884-1887

Controversy marked Prof. Aughey's departure from Nebraska and it was not long before it found him again as he took up the post of Territorial Geologist for Wyoming. In a personal interview with H. H. Bancroft on 29 March 1885 conducted in Cheyenne, Aughey stated he was appointed Territorial Geologist for Wyoming by Gov. Hale on 15 October 1883 (Bancroft Collection 1885). However, William Bryan (1986), writing on the history of the Geological Survey of Wyoming, gives the date as 15 October 1884, which he based on the Territorial Papers of Wyoming in the National Archives and two Cheyenne newspaper accounts dated 16 October 1884. No matter which date is correct, it is clear that Aughey had been working in Wyoming for a number of years, producing his first paper in 1882. On a personal note in the Bancroft interview, Aughey indicated that his wife and daughter were still living in Lincoln.

In his interview (Bancroft Collection 1885), Aughey stated that while at the University of Nebraska he made periodic trips, initially during his vacations, to Wyoming, Utah, and Colorado. Later, during terms at the University, he was occasionally absent doing geological work for the Union Pacific Railroad, particularly between Cheyenne and Salt Lake City. Just prior to becoming the Territorial Geologist, Aughey was an agent for the Wyoming Central Association, a group of oil investors. He undertook an inspection trip of the Salt Creek area and correctly predicted that it would become a great oil field (Bryan 1986). Aughey filed for a placer oil claim in Salt Creek in 1884, but by 1888 he had sold the claim to the Wyoming Central Association just as the field was developed (Wells 2005).

Bryan (1986) credits Aughey's work on the oil basins of Wyoming as being "proved uncannily accurate." He predicted after studying all the known oil basins in Wyoming that when any of the oil basins were properly worked "they will develop into magnificently paying properties." Bryan (1986) also lauded Aughey's efforts to preserve some of Wyoming's rich fossil heritage within the state. At his own expense, Aughey brought one of his students from the University of Nebraska, Wilbur C. Knight, to conduct digs in the fossil beds near Como Bluff in August and September of 1885. Based on the success of this expedition, Aughey recommended the formation of a museum for public display of the fossils and minerals, but the museum was never established.

Even with his undeniable successes in Wyoming, Aughey's time there became overshadowed by charges of salting ore samples from the Carbonate Belle Mine, which was in the Silver Crown mining district northwest of Cheyenne. Aughey's early assaying of ore from the mine reported a return of $200 of gold per ton (Hunt 1941, Bryan 1986). There were doubts of this very high assay so samples were sent to outside assayers. These results showed only traces of gold in the ore. Aughey explained the differences were due to the fact that he was using a new assaying technique. In August of 1886, Aughey was sent with ore samples to Kentucky for further testing. These results supported his earlier results, but carelessness on the part of the smelter resulted in Aughey's poisoning by lead fumes (Aughey and Aughey-Fulmer 1918) and he returned to Cheyenne quite ill. In late 1886, the owners of the Carbonate Belle sent Aughey to the resort at Hot Springs, Arkansas, to recover his health (Bryan 1986).

Aughey returned to Cheyenne in early 1887 for one last test of the ore samples, which was conducted on 4 January 1887 by Wilbur Knight. Knight was to be in the assay room alone with Aughey instructing him through the door of an adjoining room. The test returned an assay value of $105 per ton. Almost as soon as the good news spread so did the accusation that Aughey had once again salted the sample. Knight accused Aughey of placing filings from a gold coin into the sample when he entered the room to supposedly take his medication. This prompted Knight to redo the assay within two hours, proving that the earlier sample was salted (Bryan 1986). What would have been Aughey's motive in salting samples? Rumors at the time suggested that Aughey owned stock in a mine near the Carbonate Belle, which he hoped to sell for a profit.

Aughey served out his appointed term as the Wyoming Territorial Geologist, but the post ended three months later on 31 March 1887. Neither the Carbonate Belle Mine nor any of the others in the Silver Crown District proved to be the hoped for bonanza (Hunt 1941). Knight went on to a long career with the Geological Survey of Wyoming. Aughey retired, citing ill health and returned to Hot Springs, never returning to Wyoming (Bryan 1986). Louis D. Ricketts replaced Aughey as the Territorial Geologist and Mining Engineer in April 1887. His Territorial Geologist's report covering the year 1887 mentions Aughey only once (Ricketts 1888).

Aughey was appointed in 1886 to the first board of trustees of the University of Wyoming by Territorial Governor Francis E. Warren. However, on 2 May 1887, Territorial Governor Thomas Moonlight wrote to Aughey in Hot Springs, where he was convalescing, asking when he might return to the territory so that he could attend meetings and perform his duties as a Trustee of the University. Aughey wrote to Moonlight on 8 May 1887, to resign his position (Jackson 1946). Hayes (1912) claims that while a regent Aughey "chose the site for its [University of Wyoming] location and with his own hand wrote out its scheme of organization." We have found no information to support this claim and the regents did not appear to be very active during the year that Aughey served.

The Late Years—1887-1912

Hayes (1912) reported that after Aughey survived the acute poisoning he remained "for the next five years" in Hot Springs to recover from his illness. Church records show that he was associated with a church in Hot Springs during this time (Swain personal communication). However, based on a brief account in *The Goodspeed Biographical and Historical Memoirs of Western Arkansas*, published in 1891, not all of Aughey's time in Arkansas was spent in recovery.

He is listed among the "'Old Guard' who have stood by the camp in all of its trials and tribulations." The "camp" in Bear City, Montgomery Co., Arkansas, was a gold and silver mining area in the extreme eastern part of the county about 16 miles from Hot Springs. The gold and silver ore deposits in the Bear Mountain District had been declared by the state geologist in 1888 to be "non-paying":

> Prof. A. M. Beam and Samuel Aughey, old pioneers of the camp, whose implicit faith in the existence there of gold and silver in paying quantities has never wavered or faltered, have toiled on and labored earnestly for the last two years under the most trying circumstances, endeavoring to obtain a solution of the problem of how to save the values in sufficient quantities to invite the attention and investment of capital in the development of the vast mineral resources of Bear Mountain District, and their efforts seem about to be crowned with success in the discovery of what is known as the 'Beam Electric Process.' A plant has

been erected at what was formerly known as the Smith smelter, and continued runs for the last month, on various ores of the district, in quantities ranging from 200 to 1,000 pounds have been made, and our information from reliable sources up to the hour of writing this article, is that they have been entirely satisfactory to all interested.

Because of the controversy about the presence of gold, Aughey and Beam traveled to St. Louis with a delegation from Arkansas in April-May 1888. They brought samples of ore from the "Lost Louisiana Mine" to be assayed in an independent laboratory under close observations. In 19 assays, gold was found in only two, both of which were subjected to questionable handling, not unlike the issue in Wyoming (Branner 1888a). Aughey's mining career in Arkansas was curtailed in August 1888 when the Arkansas State Geologist issued the results of a geological survey that stated "We are brought to the irresistible conclusion that ignorance or fraud, or both, are at the bottom of these high gold assays" (Branner 1888b:1). We were able to find only two other mentions (1890, 1891) of Aughey in Arkansas newspapers, both referencing the incorporation of mining companies (*Daily Arkansas Gazette*, p. 4, 24 May1890; p. 2, 15 July 1891). As recently as the Arkansas Geological Commission in 2003 stated "no payable quantities of gold have been discovered in Arkansas" (http://www.state.ar.us/agc/gold.htm).

In the early 1890s, Aughey moved to Clay County, Alabama, which seems like another enigmatic action on his part given his strongly held abolitionist beliefs during the Civil War Era. The Lutheran Church records have him first in Abner and then

Lineville, Clay Co., Alabama (Swain personal communication). A search of historical records gives no indication that a Lutheran church was located in either of these towns (The Clay County Heritage Book Committee 1998). Jeanette Bergeron, Archivist, Crumley Lutheran Archives, Columbia, SC (10 October 2001) stated "there has never been a strong Lutheran presence in Alabama, the state's churches never organized into a synod structure of their own as neighboring states did." We have not found any indication of Aughey presenting sermons for any Lutheran church in Alabama, but the Ashland newspaper, *Clay County Advance,* does note in 1895 (8(51):3, 13 December) and 1897 (11(7):3, 19 February) that he presented sermons in the Methodist Church in Lineville. On the second occasion the newspaper stated "Prof. Aughey preached an interesting sermon at the Methodist church on last Sunday, and was attended by a very large audience." Aughey performed at least one marriage while in Alabama (Scott 2000). He married Jacob Moore and Julia Baker on 1 December 1895, at the residence of the bride in Lineville. Aughey is listed on the marriage license as an "Ordained Minister of Lutheran Church." Although Aughey had not given up his ministerial duties, he certainly was serving as no more than an itinerant pastor for the scattered Lutheran families in Clay County.

While in Alabama, Aughey corresponded with friends and family in Nebraska. When his wife Elizabeth discovered letters that revealed his romantic relationship with Mrs. Warner from Waverly, she sent them to friends in Waverly who in turn sent them to the *Lincoln Weekly News* for publication (EC Aughey 1894). Although the affair did not make the front page, it was a headline on page three. The love letter from Warner, dated 9

July 1894, includes phrases such as "<u>my loved one</u> [underlining in original]," "Dearest," "With more love and good wishes than tongue can tell or pen express," and "thy loving friend." Aughey and Warner must have begun their relationship in the 1870s or early 1880s when Aughey was working at the church in Waverly.

To keep their relationship a secret from their spouses, Warner received letters under the name "Mrs. Cochran" at the Waverly Post Office and Professor Aughey under the name of "Mrs. A. S. Lathrop" at the Abner Post Office. A portion of the letter printed in the newspaper is devoted to Warner's concern over the fact that Mr. Reitz, a mutual acquaintance, had been appointed postmaster in Waverly. Warner is particularly concerned that Mr. Reitz "enjoys gossip," and she considers getting a post office box at University Place [now part of northeastern Lincoln] where she goes at least once a week. Warner requests that Aughey to be careful to not post all of his letters from Abner because Mr. Reitz may become suspicious.

The remainder of the letter is devoted to topics of religion, politics, current events, weather, and Aughey's gardening. Warner even questions whether the Lord's Prayer should read "Leave us not in temptation," rather than "Lead us not into temptation." Although her comments are not specific, she is quite concerned about civil unrest, which was most likely the Pullman strike that began in Chicago in May 1894, as she worries that their letters might not be received. That Warner closes with "I heartily wish the earth would yield you as freely of her gold and silver, so that you need not remain there much longer, but return to me, who so longs and prays for a sight of my beloved," suggests that Aughey had discussed with her his work in mining and his hope of obtaining a rich return. Elizabeth Aughey's letter (1894) to her friends concluded, "Well, I don't think two old grey haired fools would run such risks to tell each other how impure and unfaithful they are to all that would make them noble personal friends." It is not known if Aughey and Warner continued as paramours. But Aughey and Elizabeth remained married for another 18 years, until Aughey's death.

While in Alabama, Aughey taught for a short time "at a small college near Birmingham, Alabama" (Hayes 1912). Beginning in 1895, Aughey served for three years on the faculty of Lineville College, in Lineville, Clay Co. (Griffin, notes received 6 November 2001). This college was chartered by the General Assembly of Alabama in 1891 and functioned until 1911, and then was chartered as the North East Alabama Agricultural and Industrial Institute, which closed in 1917. Before becoming a college, it served as a primary school for the region for many years. Lineville College was granting A.B., B.S., and Ph.B. degrees, although it appears to have had only grades 1 through 12 and would be termed a prep school today. The purpose of the college was to provide a classical education in a setting noted for health and morality. There was a strong emphasis on religion, but of no particular denomination, and temperance, which would have matched Aughey's philosophy. In the academic year 1895–96, Dr. Aughey taught German, Greek, and the sciences, in the next academic year only the sciences, and finally in 1897-98 he taught only Greek.

Aughey's arrival at Lineville College was announced in the Ashland newspaper, *People's Party Advocate*, of 2 August 1895: "Prof. Aughey comes to us with twelve years' experience in the University of Nebraska, and is undoubtedly the ripest scholar in this section of Alabama. It is only by a chain of circumstances fortunate for Lineville College that we were able to secure his services." Lineville College regularly held a Teachers Institute for area teachers. The report of the institute in the same newspaper for 6 September 1895, stated "Those present say it was the most enjoyable of any number of years. Much of the unusual interest must be attributed to the eminent scholar and Professor at Lineville College—Prof. Aughey. Since hearing learned and practical discussions, the people are at his feet." The "Lineville Chat" column in the *People's Party Advocate* of 27 September 1895, tells us "The students are unbounded in their praise of Prof. Aughey's work in the school room." At subsequent Teacher Institutes, Aughey made presentations on such subjects as "The advantages of natural history studies" (28 February 1896), "Foreign languages in public schools" (11 September 1896), "Best methods of teaching history" (28 May 1897), and "Education and citizenship" (2 February 1899). At the institute held on 14 May 1897, the main evening speech was given by Prof. Aughey on the topic of "Education as a factor in morals, government, and religion" (28 May 1897). The *People's Party Advocate* never makes a mention of Aughey's involvement with any Lutheran activities in Linesville.

Although he made a living working at the college, we believe the real reason Aughey was in Alabama was that he hoped to strike it rich. Gold was discovered as early as 1830 in Alabama—Clay County is located in a belt of northeast to southwest lying counties in eastern Alabama where gold had been discovered and mined (Adams 1930a, 1930b, Russell 1957). The gold producing counties include Chilton, Clay, Cleburne, Coosa, Randolph, Talladega, and Tallapoosa. The major gold producing years ended in 1849 when many miners left for California (Dean

1991), but gold mining was revived again in the 1880s. There is enough evidence at hand of Aughey's gold mining activity in Alabama to believe it was the primary the reason that he moved there. In the Johnson City, Tennessee, newspaper of 9 November 1893 there is an off-the-cuff description of Aughey as the "former superintendent of the Pinetucky mine" (*The Comet*, Johnson City, TN, p. 4, 19 November 1893). The Pinetucky mine was described as a small, former gold mine. The vein averaged $38 per ton in 1896 (https://thediggings.com/mines/21619). In the same article from Johnson City, Aughey was listed as the "vice president" of the newly incorporated Goldberg Mining Company, also located in Randolph Co., Alabama. This mine apparently is still in operation, producing primarily gold and arsenic (https://thediggings.com/mines/21602).

In the "Lineville Locals" section of the Ashland newspaper, *Clay County Advance*, of 26 February 1897 (11(8):3), there appeared a brief notice, "Prof. Samuel Aughey reports that gold is plentiful at the mine where he is employed." In the 1900 Alabama census, Aughey gave his occupation as "gold mining" and in response to the question "months not employed" he gave zero. Finally, a display advertisement in the *New York Times* of 18 November 1901 (page 11), placed by The Baltimore Mining and Smelting Co. mentions Prof. Aughey. The company owned the Washington Mine in Randolph Co., and the Pinetucky Gold Mine in Cleburne Co. (actually in Randolph Co., see Adams 1930b: 25-27). Part of the advertisement states:

> The celebrated Prof. Samuel Aughey, Ph. D., LL.
> D., for 12 years Geologist of the State of Nebraska
> and Territorial Geologist of Wyoming has made

a thorough examination of the property, and his report is contained in our prospectus, which is now ready.

According to Hayes (1912), Aughey and Elizabeth moved to Spokane, Washington, in 1899 to be near their daughter and grandchildren who lived in Pullman; however, Samuel Aughey is recorded in Alabama rather than Washington in the 1900 census (Alabama Census). Aughey is recorded in the Ashland Precinct of Clay County on 9 June 1900. He appears to be living alone in a rented house and Elizabeth is not recorded in this census. Lutheran church records have his address as Spokane Falls, Washington, beginning in 1903.

On 1 January 1901, Aughey was quoted in the *Spokesman Review,* unequivocally promoting a gas and oil field in northern Whitman County and to prepare a "Prospectus of the Spokane Natural Gas, Oil and Coal Co," which was issued in 1902 (Aughey 1902). The prospectus contains Aughey's usual optimistic views of the resources available on the property controlled by the company. Despite a positive report by Aughey, no oil resources were developed in the Spokane region (Johnson et al. 1997).

Rev. Hayes, who knew Aughey during his Washington years, in his eulogy (Hayes 1912) described Aughey's activities during this time:

> …there are few men in all the Pacific Northwest that have led a more strenuous life for the past 13 years than he. The scene of his labors for the most part lay far beyond the lines of railway travel. He followed the trail over precipitous mountains and down into the abysmal

depths of unexplored canyons where the forest under-
growth shut out the light of day. Vehicles were not to be
thought of; very often the way was too difficult for even
the trained and sure-footed cow-pony.

Hayes noted that for most of these travels Aughey carried with
him "nothing but his long iron staff with its hammer-like head
and chisel-shaped foot." Hayes (1912) claimed that Aughey's
travels had taken him from northern British Columbia to California and from the Pacific Ocean to Wyoming.

Hayes' eulogy interestingly explains that Aughey, now in
his late sixties and seventies, covered so much terrain on foot,
because he had been employed by men who had hired him
"to locate their mining interests." When discussing his ministerial work in these later years, Hayes (1912) writes, "He was
always giving Bibles, especially among mining men." It seems
that Aughey was never far from his mining interests and almost
certainly his primary motivation was gold. Aughey does seem
to have carried on some theological work during his Washington days. Hayes noted that "The Lutheran church in Hartline
[Grant Co., Washington] stands today as a monument to his
zeal for home missions," but the church did not survive after
the departure of several families (Aughey and Aughey-Fulmer
1918).

Aughey died on 3 February 1912, only five days short of his
eighty-first birthday [or eightieth]. Although he died in Washington State, he was interred in the old cemetery of St. Steven's
Lutheran Church near his childhood home in Pennsylvania
on land that his father had donated for the construction of the
church (Gilbert et al. 1968).

Discussion

Manley (1967:108) claimed: "One of the best examples of the 'scientific promoter' is Professor Samuel Aughey who, during his twelve years in the University of Nebraska, insisted that men, through the proper utilization of 'known scientific principles,' could make the so-called Great American Desert 'blossom as a rose.'" Manley (1967) believed that Aughey was a "boomer" for the state, meaning that he campaigned vigorously to promote the popularity of the state, "Whether discussing grasshoppers, soil or rainfall, Aughey's pronouncements, although phrased in captivating scientific jargon, contained large doses of speculation, optimism and pure hopefulness." "He had a mission—to promote settlement of the West," (Manley 1967:114-115). Manley (1967), however, believed that such actions undertaken by Aughey in support of the business interests in Nebraska, especially the railroads, had a "deleterious effect upon the rational settlement of the plains." The effects of such settlement patterns were seen as early as the 1890s when drought conditions returned to the plains.

Aughey was both a promoter for the state of Nebraska and the University. Was his promotion beyond what he really believed was appropriate and what was supported by his own research? This question can only be answered by knowing what was inside of Aughey's mind and we get no hints from the written record. Manley (1967) was particularly critical of this promotional aspect of Aughey's work and writing, but our perspective from 2020 may be quite different than Manley's perspective from the mid-1960s. Aughey was an employee of the university and the state, with such a position come certain expectations and when requests are made by state officials. Considering that in 2020 the University of Nebraska-Lincoln has a Vice Chancellor for Research and Economic Development, including the offices of Technology Development, Industry Relations, and Nebraska Innovation Campus, which is a 10-year old, 249-acre public/private research and technology center expected "to become a center of innovation and economic development for the state and the university," economic development and promotion of the state's economy seems to be an active part of the jobs of all faculty members.

Regents at the University of Nebraska must have felt fortunate that Samuel Aughey was available to fill its faculty position in natural sciences given that the primary criterion for becoming a faculty member was to be an ordained minister and positions in the natural science were often filled by Lutherans. Aughey worked hard in the time that he was at the University. His teaching load was extremely heavy—teaching, at both the university and prep school levels, a full range of natural science courses plus drawing, agriculture, German, Cicero, and Virgil. By our count, there were 28 different-titled courses for the university and 7 for the Latin school (Table 1). In 1875–76, Aughey taught 6 college courses and 2 in the Latin school, and later in 1880-1881 he taught 9 courses for the University. His teaching method seemed to be primarily lectures, which many of the students appreciated. Throughout his lifetime, his oratory skills were universally lauded. In fact, student complaints about Aughey only surfaced late in his time at the university when he was spending more and more time away from campus doing service work.

Aughey also carried a heavy service load in addition to teaching for the University, which was probably an activity that had been unanticipated as the University was established. However, shortly after coming to the University natural history materials and specimens started arriving for him to identify—soil, chemicals, rocks, flora, and fauna. To do this work, takes time, equipment, and reference materials; and proper analyses depend on all three of these factors. Without detailed knowledge of Aughey's methods and practices it is difficult to assess the quality of his scientific work in its historic context. Other services provided by Aughey dealt with regional natural resources such as coal, migratory locusts, ground water, and work for the railroads and the early petroleum industry. His work in the petroleum industry appears to have been accurate and useful, and his scientific work, at the very least, provided instructive information for the researchers who followed him.

As stated previously, it is Aughey's research that has come under the greatest criticism. It is our belief that some of this criticism is well deserved, but some of his work does not appear as poor when viewed in its proper historic context. Aughey's research was primarily observational. He was not testing a hypothesis and most of the observations were not placed in a larger context. Aughey was primarily a compiler of scientific information. His publications are clearly the result of his searching the available literature for information that might be applied to Nebraska, and mingling this information with his own observations. One of the unfortunate problems is that Aughey's observations can't be distinguished from those gleaned from the literature. It is clear that Aughey's publications belong to an earlier age of amateur naturalists. Even when compared with the work of outstanding naturalists from this earlier period, including John Bachman, Thomas Nuttall, Thomas Say, and Alexander Wilson, his work does not measure up to their standards. Aughey's amateur work lacks the insights, understandings, cognitive coherence, and integrative views of the earlier professional naturalists.

Placing Aughey and his work in the broader context of what was happening in 1860s and 1870s in American science allows for a better understanding of the basis for the current criticism of his research. The amateur natural historian was slowly being replaced by the trained specialist in the sciences during this period. It was from the tradition of the physician-naturalist, pastor-naturalist, and others who pursued natural history as a secondary avocation that modern biology was emerging in the 1840s and 1850s (Benson 1986). Aughey was from this older tradition. His formal training in science was obtained at Pennsylvania College as he was preparing to enter the ministry. The remainder of his education came from informal sources such as reading, studying nature, and interacting with other naturalists. By the 1870s, Harvard and Yale universities were offering advanced degrees and other American students were going to Europe, especially Germany and England, for advanced studies in the sciences (Benson 1986). With the publication of Darwin's, *Origin of Species*, in 1859, the revolution in biology was rapidly propelled forward to never return to its old form; however, this change occurred over a generation and did not proceed at the same rate everywhere.

Daniels (1967) details the professionalization of American science in the nineteenth century, and the University of Nebraska was no exception. Even before Aughey took up his position at the new University of Nebraska, a gathering wave of people were receiving specialized training in science. This changed science, including biology, forever, forming the roots of modern science. Although this was occurring in academia around Aughey, he was clearly so immersed in his daily duties that he was untouched and perhaps unaware of these changes. The first phase in the professionalization in Daniels' system is preemption." In "this phase a set of knowledge becomes exclusive to a particular group and is not part of general knowledge. This exclusive knowledge must be obtained through specialized training and education. In natural history and biology, this transition occurred when the natural system of classification based in Darwinian ideals came into use.

During this "preemptive" phase in science, the term "scientist" came into use and the term "popularizer" was applied to those delivering scientific information to broad audiences but not creating new knowledge. Indeed, the term "popularizer" accurately describes Aughey's work at Nebraska. He was compiling scientific information about Nebraska and working to make this information available and meaningful to citizens of the state. Only a small portion of this information was based on Aughey's original research. In fact, if Aughey's contributions were to be assessed based on a modern land grant university system, it would fit the work of an extension faculty member or educator. He gathered scientific information in service to the needs of the citizens of the state, especially in the area of agricultural development. This work is still an important function of modern land grant universities.

The next important phase in Daniels (1967) professionalization of science was "institutionalization," which was a time filled with conflict. University-educated professionals, the new holders of the essential information, guarded against amateur interlopers and weeded them out with charges of "thoroughly dishonest," "extrascientific considerations," and "charlatanism." Immediately upon Aughey's departure from the university, the position in natural sciences was split and was filled by Lewis E. Hicks and Charles E. Bessey in 1884 and in 1891 Erwin H. Barbour arrived to replace Hicks. Both Hicks and Bessey had master's degrees from their home institutions, respectively, Dennison University, and Michigan State University. . Hicks also worked with Louis Agassiz at Harvard and Bessey worked with Asa Gray at Harvard. Hicks had taught for 14 years at Dennison University and Bessey for 15 years at Iowa State University. Barbour arrived with a Ph.D. from Yale doing work with O. C. Marsh and J. D. Dana. The contrast between the qualifications held by this new professionalized cadre of scientists and Aughey's qualifications could not be sharper. These scientists followed areas of specialized research—geology, botany, and vertebrate paleontology, respectively.

These dramatic changes at the University of Nebraska occurred in just a 20-year period. In fact, it was one of Bessey's students (Pound 1894) that leveled the charge of charlatanism against Aughey's work. Clearly not only had there been a change in personnel at Nebraska but these changes were being institutionalized by hiring only professionalized scientists, and Aughey and his work were now outside of this group. The other two phases—"legitimation" and "professional autonomy"—identified by Daniels (1967) also impacted Nebraska, but by then Aughey was only a distant memory.

The initial goal of our investigation was to gain a better understanding of the contributions of Samuel Aughey, and to solve in some way the apparent enigma of his life. The archival research gathered here provides a more in-depth and nuanced understanding of Aughey's scientific work and his overall career. Yet, we cannot claim to have solved all of the mysteries that made Aughey's life so enigmatic. As an ordained minister, he was sworn to serve others, yet he engaged in land speculation, questionable business dealings involving borrowed money, short-term oil claims, and ultimately, he was tempted by gold and silver and the promise of great personal wealth, which he relentlessly pursued for 25 years until his death. And he was involved for more than a decade in a romantic relationship with a married parishioner. The longest that he stayed at any position was the 12 years he was at the University of Nebraska. He usually left his jobs abruptly because of an illness that was never quite explained.

His behavior certainly defied social norms, and as such may have led historians to question his character and his work equally. Most troubling are the distortions, exaggerations and ultimately fabricated claims made about Samuel Aughey in the historic record. To be sure, Aughey worked to bolster his own record with falsehoods. Yet, the direct result of historians promoting and not fact checking negative and false claims is they have obscured and made it difficult to assess Aughey's true record.

We feel that our overall assessment of Samuel Aughey is best articulated by two of his contemporaries. His former student Lawrence A. Bruner (Taylor 1931) who became an international expert on migratory locusts and related orthopterans wrote that "He was a hard worker. His work was earnest and sincere, but with so much put upon him, scientific exactness could scarcely be expected." Finally, Charles E. Bessey (1912), Nebraska's outstanding scientist and an internationally recognized scholar of plant classification, wrote in Aughey's obituary: "Let us honor him for his scientific spirit which he maintained here in the day when science was small and weak, and which he carried to the end of his long life."

Acknowledgements

We thank the staff of the Library and Archives Division, Nebraska State Historical Society; Joseph Svoboda and later Mary Ellen Ducey and the staff of the University of Nebraska Archives; Vivian Peterson, Evangelical Lutheran Church in America, Nebraska Synod; George Corner, University of Nebraska State Museum; David Hedrick, Gettysburg College; Lisa Seivert, Buffalo Museum of Science; Peg Dalton, Wittenburg University; Bob Schmidt, Miami University Archives; Doug McCabe, Ohio University; Tammy L. Peters, Smithsonian Institution Archives; Craig Ludwig, National Museum of Natural History; Jeanette Bergeron, Crumley Lutheran Archives, Columbia, SC; Rai Goerler, Ohio State University; Ellen D. Swain, Evangelical Lutheran Church of America for access to their archives and assistance in research on Aughey. A special thank you to Herbert E. Griffin, Oxford, AL, for sharing his information and insights on Lineville College. We appreciate the work over several years of the Interlibrary Loan Service, Love Library, University of Nebraska-Lincoln, in finding and obtaining for our use the most obscure literature needed for this research.

Angie Fox, Exhibit Coordinator and Scientific Illustrator for the University of Nebraska State Museum, prepared and made available the four images used as figures. We appreciate her continued professional work on images for our publications. These images are from the Erwin H. Barbour, Museum Photographs Series (RG 32-01-01), Archives & Special Collections, University of Nebraska–Lincoln Libraries. For permission to use these images, we thank Susan J. Weller, Director, University of Nebraska State Museum, University of Nebraska-Lincoln.

Literature Cited

Books and Journals

[All known publications of Samuel Aughey have been gathered in Appendix 1 and are not repeated here to save space and duplication. Please check Samuel Aughey's bibliography in Appendix 1 for all in-text citations to his work.]

Adams GI. (1930a) A century of gold mining in Alabama. *Alabama Historical Quarterly* 1: 271-279.

Adams GI. (1930b) Gold deposits of Alabama and occurrences of copper, pyrite, arsenic and tin. *Bulletin of the Geological Survey of Alabama* 40: 1-91.

Allan JT, editor. (1885) *Annual report of the Nebraska State Horticultural Society, 1883* (Lincoln, Nebraska: Journal Company, State Printers).

Andreas AT. (1882) *History of the state of Nebraska; containing a full account of its growth from an uninhabited territory to a wealthy and important state; of its early settlements rapid increase in population, and the marvellous development of its great natural resources. Also an extended description of its counties, cities, towns and villages, their advantages, industries, manufactures and commerce; biographical sketches, portraits of prominent men and early settlers; views of residences and business blocks, cities and towns* (Chicago: The Western Historical Company, 1506 pp).

Anonymous. (1874) Poisonous liquors—Prof. Aughey's analysis and report. *Yankton Press and Union and Dakotaian* Yankton, South Dakota, 28 May.

Anonymous. (1912) Former Lincoln man dead. *State Journal* Lincoln, Nebraska, 10 February.

Anonymous. (1978) Mrs. Lamb's bequest for scholarships recalls Prof. Aughey's unusual life. *Nebraska Campaign Reporter, University of Nebraska Foundation*, No. 5, March.

Armstrong WJ. (1883) The case of Prof. Aughey: a summing up of the investigation so far as it has progressed. *Nebraska State Journal,* p. 3, 25 August.

Aughey EC. (1894) Loved each other and both are married but not to each other. *Lincoln Weekly News* 9 (49):3, 23 August.

Aughey EC, and Aughey-Fulmer HB. (1918) Rev. Samuel Aughey, Ph.D., LL.D. In WHB Carney (Editor), *History of the Alleghany Evangelical Lutheran Synod of Pennsylvania,* pp. 220-224 (Philadelphia: Lutheran Publication Society, 1: xii + 1-454).

Barbour EH. (1908) Report on the Honey Creek Coal Mine. *Publication of the Nebraska Geological Survey* 2: 353-364.

Benson KR. (1986) Concluding remarks: American natural history and biology in the nineteenth century. *American Zoologist* 26: 381-384.

Benton AR. (1872a) *The register and catalogue of the University of Nebraska, Lincoln, Nebraska. First Session, 1871-72* (Lincoln: Randall & Smail, Book and Job Printers).

Benton AR. (1872b) *Report to the Board of Regents and address, by A. R. Benton, Chancellor, University of Nebraska, 1871-72* (Lincoln: State Journal Printer).

Benton AR. (1873) *The register and catalogue of the University of Nebraska, Lincoln, Nebraska. Second Session, 1872-73* (Lincoln: The Statesman Book and Job Print).

Benton AR. (1874a) *The register and catalogue of the University of Nebraska, Lincoln, Nebraska. Third Session, 1873-74* (Lincoln: Journal Company, State Printers).

Benton AR. (1874b) *Chancellor's report to the Board of Regents for the academic year, ending June 24th, 1874* (Lincoln: Journal Company, State Printers).

Benton AR. (1875a) *The register and catalogue of the University of Nebraska, Lincoln, Nebraska. Fourth Session, 1874-75* (Lincoln: Journal Company, State Printers).

Benton AR. (1875b) *The Chancellor's report for the fourth session of the University of Nebraska, ending June 23d, 1875* (Lincoln: Journal Company, State Printers).

LITERATURE CITED

Benton AR. (1876) *The Chancellor's report to the Board of Regents for the academic year ending June 22d, 1876* (Lincoln: Journal Company, State Printers).

Bessey CE. (1880) *Proceedings of the Iowa Academy of Sciences, 1875-80* (Iowa City: John P. Irish, 28 pp).

Bessey CE. (1912) Professor Doctor Samuel Aughey: born February 8, 1831; died February 3, 1912. *The University Journal* 9(2): 19-20.

Bolick MR. (1993) Samuel Aughey, Jr.: the controversial first director of the University of Nebraska State Museum. *Museum Notes, University of Nebraska State Museum* 84: 1-4.

Branner JC. (1888a) Gigantic frauds: startling report on the gold and silver mines. *Daily Arkansas Gazette*, Little Rock, p. 1, 9 August.

Branner JC. (1888b) No gold in Arkansas. *Fayetteville Weekly Democrat*, Fayetteville, Arkansas, p. 1, 17 August.

Bryan W. (1986) A history of the Geological Survey of Wyoming. *Bulletin of the Geological Survey of Wyoming* 65: ix + 1-125.

Call RE. (1892) *Proceedings of the Iowa Academy of Sciences for 1887, 1888, 1889* (Des Moines: R. E. Adams, Printer, 101 pp).

Daniels GH. (1967) The process of professionalization in American science: the emergent period, 1820-1860. *Isis* 58: 150-166.

Dean LS. (1991) Alabama gold: golden harvest of the Piedmont. *Alabama Heritage* summer, pp. 20-29.

Diffendal AP. (1976) Nebraska in the Centennial Exposition at Philadelphia, 1876. *Nebraska History* 57: 69-81.

Diffendal AP. (1978) A centennial history of the Nebraska State Historical Society, 1878-1978. *Nebraska History* 59: 311-329, 429-437.

Edmunds AC. (1871) *Pen sketches of Nebraskans with photographs* (Omaha: R. & J. Wilbur, Stationers, 510 pp).

Fairfield EB. (1876) *Fifth annual register and catalogue of the University of Nebraska, Lincoln, Nebraska* (Lincoln: Journal Company, State Printers).

Fairfield EB. (1877) *Sixth annual register and catalogue of the University of Nebraska, Lincoln, Nebraska* (Lincoln: Journal Company, State Printers).

Fairfield EB. (1878) *Seventh annual register and catalogue of the University of Nebraska, Lincoln, Nebraska* (Lincoln: Journal Company, State Printers).

Fairfield EB. (1879) *Eighth annual register and catalogue of the University of Nebraska, Lincoln, Nebraska* (Lincoln: Journal Company, State Printers).

Fairfield EB. (1880) *Ninth annual register and catalogue of the University of Nebraska, Lincoln, Nebraska* (Lincoln: Journal Company, State Printers).

Fairfield EB. (1882) *Tenth annual catalogue of the University of Nebraska, Lincoln, Nebraska, for the academic year 1881-2 with announcements of the courses of study in the different departments for the year 1882-3* (Lincoln: State Journal Company).

Florence CA, Gibson J, and Buchanan JR. (1883) *Northern Nebraska, considered geographically, topographically, geologically and experimentally, showing the chances for investment in the eastern parts and for free homes in the west, the country traversed by the Sioux City & Pacific Railroad* (Battle Creek, Michigan: Review & Herald Steam Printing House).

Foster M. (1994) *Strange genius: the life of Ferdinand Vandeveer Hayden* (Niwot, Colorado: Roberts Rinehart Publishers, xv + 443 pp).

Furnas RW, editor. (1877) *Transactions of the Nebraska State Horticultural Society for the year 1877* (Lincoln: Journal Company, State Printers, 125 pp).

Furnas RW, editor. (1879) *Annual reports of the Nebraska State Horticultural Society, 1878 and 1879* (Lincoln: Journal Company, State Printers, 150 pp).

Furnas RW, editor. (1885) *Transactions and reports of the Nebraska State Historical Society* (Lincoln: State Journal Co., State Printers, vol. 1: 1-233).

Genoways T. (1989) Coal, coal, coal! *Nebraskaland Magazine* 67(10): 15-17.

Gilbert HS, Flack LH, and Olson VH. (1968) *The Heikes-Aughey family history and register of descendants* (Wayne, Nebraska: privately published for the authors by Wayne Herald, 199 pp).

LITERATURE CITED

Hayden FV. (1868) Remarks on the possibility of a workable bed of coal in Nebraska. *American Journal of Science* 40:326-330.

Hayden FV. (1871) *Preliminary report of the U. S. Geological Survey of Wyoming and portions of contiguous territories* (Washington, DC: U. S. Printing Office, pp. 7-8).

Hayes WGM. (1912) Prof. Samuel Aughey lived a useful life. *The Pullman Herald,* Pullman, Washington, 23 February, p. 3.

Hitchcock HE. (1883) *Eleventh annual catalogue of the University of Nebraska for the academic year 1882-3* (Lincoln: Journal Company, State Printers).

Hoke E. (2000) A critical review of the Unionoid mollusks reported for Nebraska by Samuel Aughey (1877). *Central Plains Archeology* 8: 35-47.

Hoke E. (2005) The unionid mussels (Mollusca: Bivalvia: Unionidae) of the Big Blue River basin of northeastern Kansas and southeastern Nebraska. *Transactions of the Nebraska Academy of Sciences* 30: 33-57.

Hoke E. (2011) The freshwater mussels (Mollusca: Bivalva: Unionoida) of Nebraska. *Transactions of the Nebraska Academy of Sciences* 32: 1-32.

Howard GE. (1919) Early faculty and equipment. *Semi-centennial anniversary book: the University of Nebraska,* pp. 24-29 (Lincoln: University of Nebraska 144 pp).

Hunt LC. (1941) *Wyoming: a guide to its history, highways, and people* (New York: Oxford University Press, 490 pp).

Jackson WT. (1946) The administration of Thomas Moonlight 1887-1889. *Annals of Wyoming* 18: 139-162.

Johnson H. (1880) *Johnson's history of Nebraska* (Omaha: Herald Printing House, xvi + 591).

Johnson SY, Tennyson ME, Lingley WS Jr, and Law BE. (1997) Petroleum geology of the state of Washington. *U. S. Geological Survey Professional Paper* 1582: iv + 1-40.

Kennedy J. (1977) Aughey's spirit lingers on. "Education Log" column. *Sunday Journal and Star,* Lincoln, Nebraska, 6 February.

Knoll RE. (1995) *Prairie university: a history of the University of Nebraska* (Lincoln: University of Nebraska Press, xviii + 223 pp).

Kollmorgen W. (1935) Rainmakers on the plains. *Scientific Monthly* 40: 146-152.

Leidy J. (1853) The ancient fauna of Nebraska or, a description of remains of extinct Mammalia and Chelonia, from the Mauvaises Terres of Nebraska. *Smithsonian Contributions to Knowledge* 6: 1-126.

Libecap GD, and Hansen ZK. (2002) "Rain follows the plow" and dry farming doctrine: the climate information problem and homestead failure in the upper Great Plains, 1890-1925. *Journal of Economic History* 62: 86-120.

Lund LD. (1990) *Kountze Memorial Lutheran Church in Omaha: a history* (Privately published, iv + 174 pp).

Manley RN. (1967) Samuel Aughey: Nebraska's scientific promoter. *Journal of the West* 6: 108-118.

McBride JC, editor. (1878) Portrait page: Professor Samuel Aughey. *The Nebraska Farmer* 2 (5): 74.

McGee WJ. (1889) Paleolithic man in America: his antiquity and environment. *Popular Science Monthly* 34: 20-36.

Merrill GP. (1920) Contributions to a history of American state geological and natural history surveys. *Bulletin of the United States National Museum* 109: xvii + 1-549.

Merrill GP. (1924) *The first one hundred years of American geology* (New Haven, Connecticut: Yale University Press).

Morton JS. (1906) *Illustrated history of Nebraska: a history of Nebraska from the earliest explorations of the Trans-Mississippi region* (Lincoln: Jacob North & Company, 2: xii + 1-794).

Nebraska Academy of Sciences. (1880a) *Constitution and by-laws of the Nebraska Academy of Sciences, adopted January 30th, 1880* (Omaha: Republican Book and Job Printing House, 15 pp).

Nebraska Academy of Sciences. (1880b) *Academy of Sciences* [circular] (Omaha: Nebraska Academy of Sciences, 3 pp).

Nipher FE. (1886) *The Transactions of the Academy of Science of St. Louis* (St. Louis: R. P. Studley & Co., 4[1878-1886]: 18 + xii + 688 + cxxxiv + 12 + 10 + 8 + 16).

Owen DD. (1852*) Report of the Geological Survey of Wisconsin, Iowa, and Minnesota; and incidentally of a portion of Nebraska Territory. Made under instructions from the United State Treasury Department* (Philadelphia: Lippincott, Grambo & Co., xxxviii + 638 pp).

Pound L. (1946) Nebraska rain lore and rain making. *California Folklore Quarterly* 5: 129-142.

Pound R. (1894) Flora of Nebraska—Synchytria, Mucoraceae, and Entomophthoraceae of Nebraska. *Botanical Seminar, University of Nebraska* Part 1: 35-53.

Powell JW. (1878) *Report of the methods of surveying the Public Domain, to the Secretary of the Interior, at the request of the National Academy of Sciences* (Washington, DC: Government Printing Office, 16 pp.

Powell JW. (1879) *Report on the lands of the arid region of the United States: with a more detailed account of the lands of Utah. Geographical and Geological Survey of the Rocky Mountain Region* (Washington, DC: Government Printing Office, xv + 195 pp).

Ricketts LD. (1888) *Annual report of the Territorial Geologist to the Governor of Wyoming—January 1888* (Cheyenne: The Leader Book and Job Printing House, 87 pp).

Riley CV. (1878a) *The Transactions of the Academy of Science of St. Louis* (St. Louis: R. P. Studley Company, 3[1868-1877]: x + 602 + cclxxxvi + 8 + 5 + 8 + 10).

Riley CV, editor. (1878b) *First annual report of the United States Entomological Commission for the year 1877 relating to the Rocky Mountain locust and the best methods of preventing its injuries and of guarding against its invasions, in pursuance of an appropriation made by Congress for this purpose* (Washington, DC: Government Printing Office, 477 + [295] pp).

Rivinus EF, and Youssef EM. (1992) *Spencer Baird of the Smithsonian* (Washington, DC: Smithsonian Institution Press, x +228 pp).

Ross LS. (1918) *Proceedings of the Iowa Academy of Science for 1918* (Des Moines: The State of Iowa, volume 25).

Russell RA. (1957) Gold mining in Alabama before 1860. *The Alabama Review* 10: 5-14.

Sailors G. (1958) *Dakota City Centennial, 1858-1958* (Dakota City, Nebraska: Centennial Book Committee, 53 pp).

Schott CA. (1872) Tables and results of the precipitation, in rain and snow, in the United States: and at some stations in adjacent parts of North America, and in Central and South America. Collected by the Smithsonian Institution, and discussed under the direction of Joseph Henry, secretary. *Smithsonian Contributions to Knowledge* 18 (art. 2): iii + 1-175.

Schott CA. (1876) Tables, distribution, and variations of the atmospheric temperature in the United States, and some adjacent parts of America. Collected by the Smithsonian Institution, and discussed under the direction of Joseph Henry, secretary. *Smithsonian Contributions to Knowledge* 21 (art. 5): xvi + 1-345.

Schott CA. (1881) Tables and results of the precipitation, in rain and snow, in the United States: and at some stations in adjacent parts of North America, and in Central and South America. Collected by the Smithsonian Institution, and discussed under the direction of Joseph Henry and Spenser F. Baird, secretaries. *Smithsonian Contributions to Knowledge* 24 (art. 2): xx + 1-249.

Schultz CB. (1982) A preliminary history of the Nebraska Academy of Sciences, 1880-1982. *Transactions of the Nebraska Academy of Sciences* 10: 1-4.

Schultz CB. (1986). Founders and presidents of the Nebraska Academy of Sciences, 1880-1986. *Transactions of the Nebraska Academy of Sciences* 14: 1-5.

Scott PA. (2000) Marriages, Clay County, Alabama, Book F—January 5, 1895-August 17, 1898. Retrieved at <http://ftp.rootsweb.com/pub/usgenweb/al/clay/vital/marriage/claybkf.txt> on 15 August 2003.

Smith HN. (1947) Rain follows the plow: the notion of increased rainfall for the Great Plains, 1844-1880. *The Huntington Library Quarterly* 10: 169-193.

Stone JA. (1952) Disposition of public domain in Wayne County, Nebraska, 1868-1893. M. A. Thesis, University of Nebraska-Lincoln, 73 pp.

Swanberg SE. (2019) "The way of the rain": towards a conceptual framework for the retrospective examination of historical American and Australian "Rain follows the plow/plough" messages. *International Review of Environmental History* 5: 67-95.

Stover CB, and Beachem CW. (1932) The alumni record of Gettysburg College, 1832-1932 (Gettysburg, Pennsylvania: Gettysburg College).

Swenk MH. (1937) In memoriam--Lawrence Bruner. *The Nebraska Bird Review* 5: 35-48.

Taylor Mrs. HJ. (1931) Pioneers in economic ornithology. *Wilson Bulletin* 43: 177-189.

The Clay County Heritage Book Committee. (1998) *The heritage of Clay County, Alabama* (Clanton, Alabama: Heritage Publishing Consultants, Inc.).

Warner MM. (1893) *Warner's history of Dakota County, Nebraska, from the days of the pioneers and first settlers to the present time, with biographical sketches, and anecdotes of ye olden times* (Lyons, Nebraska: Lyons Mirror Job Office).

Watkins A. (1913) *History of Nebraska from the earliest explorations to the present time with portraits, maps, and tables* (Lincoln: Western Publishing and Engraving Company, vol. 3, ix + 755 pp).

Webber HJ. (1890) *Catalogue of the flora of Nebraska. Protophyta – Anthophyta* (Lincoln: Report of the Nebraska State Board of Agriculture for 1889, pp. 35-162).

Wells B, editor. (2005) Wyoming oil pioneers. *The Petroleum Age, American Oil and Gas Historical Society* 2(4): 9-11.

Wentz AR. (1927) *History of the Gettysburg Theological Seminary of the General Synod of the Evangelical Lutheran Church in the United States and of the United Lutheran Church in America, Gettysburg, Pennsylvania, 1826-1926* (Philadelphia: United Lutheran Publication House, 624 pp).

White CA, Aughey S, and Beach H. (1882) Artesian wells upon the Great Plains; being the report of the geological commission appointed to examine a portion of the Great Plains east of the Rocky Mountains, and report upon the localities deemed most favorable for experimental borings. *Departmental Report, U. S. Department of Agriculture* 19: 1-38.

Wilber CD. (1881a) Evolution: as expounded by Tyndall, Huxley and Aughey, it teaches theism. *Nebraska State Journal*, Lincoln, Nebraska, p. 2, 19 April.

Wilber CD. (1881b) *The great valleys and prairies of Nebraska and the Northwest* (Omaha: Daily Republican Printer, 382 pp).

Wolff LJ. (1950) *Story of the Midwest Synod, U. L. C. A., 1890-1950* (United Lutheran Church in America, Synod in the Midwest, 378 pp).

Worster D. (2001) *A river running west: the life of John Wesley Powell* (New York: Oxford University Press, xiii + 673 pp).

Newspapers
[newspapers cited here are available through <newspapers.com>]

Blue Valley Blade, Seward, Nebraska
    pp. 1, 4, 8 April 1880, "The Teachers in Council"
Clay County Advance, Ashland, Alabama, newspaper, vols. 1-8,
    6 January 1888 to 12 March 1897.
Columbus Era, Columbus, Nebraska
    p. 4, 11 May 1878, "Tried as by Fire"
Daily Arkansas Gazette, Little Rock, Arkansas
    p. 4, 24 May 1890, untitled
    p. 2, 15 July 1891, "New Corporations"

LITERATURE CITED

Daily Nebraska Press, Nebraska City, Nebraska
    p. 2, 25 March 1876, "The Chancellorship of the University"
Dakota City Mail, Dakota City, Nebraska
    p. 1, 14 April 1871, "Dakota County"
    p. 3, 1 September 1871, "Notice of Dissolution"
Des Moines Register, Des Moines, Iowa.
    p. 3, 19 February 1879, "Academy of Science Meeting Last Night"
Falls City Journal, Falls City, Nebraska
    p. 3, 24 June 1875, untitled
Fremont Weekly Herald, Fremont, Nebraska
    p. 6, 16 August 1883, untitled
Juniata Sentinel and Republican, Mifflintown, Pennsylvania
    p. 3, 31 July1878, untitled
Kearney Junction Times, Kearney , Nebraska
    p. 3, 29 January 1874, "Our State University"
Lincoln Daily Globe, Lincoln, Nebraska
    p. 4, 11 November 1880, untitled
Lincoln Journal Star, Lincoln, Nebraska
    p. 1, 28 July 1883. "A Mighty Fall!"
Nebraska Advertiser, Brownville, Nebraska
    p. 2, 1 May 1873, "Doctors Disagree"
    p. 2, 1 July 1875, "The Grasshopper--Results"
    p. 3, 4 November 1880, "Scott's Hog Cure"
Nebraska City News, Nebraska City, Nebraska
    p. 1, 13 June 1874, "Our State Agricultural College"
    p. 2, 27 February 1875, "The State University"
Nebraska State Journal, Lincoln, Nebraska
    p. 3, 8 June 1872, "Further Proceedings of the Lincoln Hospital Association"
    p. 4, 24 June 1874, "The Board of Regents: Their Eighteenth Session at the University Yesterday"
    p. 2, 25 June 1875, "Locusts - Parasites and Methods of Killing"
    p. 4, 25 June 1875, untitled

p. 1, 3 September 1875, "Grasshopper Commission"

p. 4, 15 June 1877, "Nothing to Fear: That's What Professors Thomas and Aughey Say Concerning the Grasshoppers"

p. 2, 15 June 1880, "The Trial of Minard for Alleged Administration of Poison"

p. 4, 16 October 1880, untitled

p. 7, 18 August 1883, "Prof. Aughey's Resignation"

p. 2, 25 August 1883, untitled

p. 3, 10 November 1883, untitled

New York Times

p. 11, 18 November 1901, untitled, display advertisement

Omaha Daily Bee, Omaha, Nebraska

p. 2, 15 May 1880, untitled

p. 2, 2 June 1880, untitled

p. 2, 17 January 1881, untitled

p. 4, 30 January 1882, "The University"

p. 4, 9 July 1883, "An Expert on Paving"

p. 4, 11 July 1883, "A Disgrace to the State"

p. 5, 28 July 1883, "Save Me from My Friend: Professor Aughey Compromised by the Skillful Forgeries of a Friend"

p. 4, 21 November 1883, "Vindicated"

Omaha Evening Bee, Omaha, Nebraska

p. 2, 5 December 1878, "Professor Aughey"

p. 2, 5 January 1880, "Preferred Candidate"

p. 2, 5 April 1880, "Talking Teachers"

Omaha Herald, Omaha, Nebraska

p. 4, 15 June 1871, "Board of Regents"

p. 2, 24 August 1871, "Our Dakota County Letter"

People's Party Advocate, Ashland, Alabama, newspaper, vols. 1-8, 7 April 1893 to 22 November 1900.

Red Cloud Chief, Red Cloud, Nebraska

p. 4, 26 February 1880, "Rainfall in Nebraska"

Sioux City Journal, Sioux City, Iowa.

1(43):3, 1 July 1865, "North Nebraska Sherds"

1(44):3, 8 July 1865, "The 4th at Dakota City"

LITERATURE CITED

    1(51):3, 2 September 1865, "North Nebraska Sherds"
    2(16):3, 13 January 1866, "Dakota County, Jan. 9, 1866"
    2(18):3, 27 January 1866, North Nebraska Sherds"
    2(21):3, 17 February 1866, "Mr. Aughey's Lecture"
    2(28):3, 7 April 7 1866, "North Nebraska Sherds"
    3(23):3, 13 April 1867, "Temperance Lecture"
Spokesman Review, Spokane, Washington
    p. 7, 1 January 1901, "Oil Near Pullman"
The Comet, Johnson City, Tennessee
    p. 4, 9 November 1893. "Rich Deposits of Gold"
The Enterprise, Pawnee City, Nebraska
    p. 2, 7 January 1880, untitled
The Independent, Wahoo, Nebraska
    p. 3, 10 June 1880, untitled
Weekly State Democrat, Lincoln, Nebraska
    p. 2, 11 June 1880, untitled
West Point Republican, West Point, Nebraska
    p. 1, 8 May 1873, "Coal in Nebraska"

Archives

University of California, Berkeley
Microfilm P-M 30. H. H. Bancroft Collection, Bancroft Library,
    University of California, Berkeley, CA 94720. Dictation taken
    during an interview with Samuel Aughey in Cheyenne,
    Wyoming, 29 March 1885.

Smithsonian Institution
Office of the Secretary Outgoing Correspondence 1865-1891.
    RU 33, Vol. 118, p. 118. Letter signed "Secretary" to Prof.
    Samuel Aughey, 4 February 1882.
Accession logbook, "1882 Additions to Collections of the
    Smithsonian Institution." Page beginning with date of
    February 3.

Office of the Secretary (Henry, Baird) 1863-1879. RU 26, Box 68, no.
274. Letter from Sam'l Aughey to Dr. F. V. Hayden, 16 January
1876.
George P. Merrill Photographic File. RU 7177, Box 1. Letters
from Sam'l Aughey to Dr. F. V. Hayden, 11 November 1875,
photograph included.

U. S. National Archives
U. S. Geological and Geographical Survey of the Territories. M623,
Roll 5, Record Group 57. Letters 1871-1879 (AB). Two letters
from Samuel Aughey to F. V. Hayden, dated 24 September 1875
and 7 July 1876.

University of Nebraska-Lincoln Libraries Archives
50/0/0
2/20 1871-1890
1/1/1, Box 2, F. 26; Box 3, F. 30; Box 4, F. 38; Box 4, F. 42; Box 4, F. 46
0/7 1871-83
2/9/1 General Correspondence
Hesperian Student, University of Nebraska, Lincoln, student
newspaper, vols. 1-12, 1871-1883

Nebraska State Historical Society
RS 3869AM, Account Book, handwritten by Samuel Aughey, Jr.
RG 3868AM
Lancaster County District Court, Appearance Docket "L,"
pp. 187-190
Lancaster County District Court, Journal "I," p. 611

Alabama Census
1900. Clay Co., Ashland Precinct. Supervisor's District No. 4,
Enumeration District 108, Sheet No. 8, p. 71.

LITERATURE CITED

Personal Communications

*[Copies of these communications will be deposited in Archives & Special
Collections, University of Nebraska–Lincoln Libraries]*

Bergeron, Jeanette. Archivist, Crumley Lutheran Archives, Columbia,
South Carolina. Electronic message to Genoways, 10 October
2001.

Dalton, Peg. Archivist, Wittenberg College, Wittenberg, Ohio.
Electronic message to Genoways, 2 September 1997; Electronic
message to Genoways, 3 September 1997.

Goerler, Rai. Archivist, Ohio State University, Columbus, Ohio.
Electronic message to Genoways, 2 September 1997.

Griffin, H. E., Jr., P. O. Box 3665, Oxford, Alabama 36203. Notes
on Lineville College based on original copies of the college
catalogue, received 6 November 2001.

Hedric, David. Special Collections Librarian, Gettysburg College,
Gettysburg, PA. Electronic message to Genoways, 2 July 1997;
Electronic message to Genoways, 3 August 1998.

McCabe, Doug. University Records Manager, Ohio University,
Athens, Ohio. Electronic message to Genoways, 30 July 1997.

Peters, Tammy L. Assistant Archivist, Office of Smithsonian
Institution Archives, Washington, DC. Letter to Genoways,
undated #1, but received between 3 September 1997 and 17
September 1997; Letter to Genoways, undated #2, but received
between 3 September 1997 and 17 September 1997; Letter to
Genoways, 17 September 1997.

Schmidt, Bob. Archivist, Miami University, Oxford, Ohio. Electronic
message to Genoways, 12 August 1997.

Swain, Ellen D. Assistant Archivist, Evangelical Lutheran Church of
America. Electronic message to Bolick, 23 November 1998.

Websites

U. S. Census online for 1900 from <www.genealogy.com >.
Arkansas Gold online <www.state.ar.us/agc/gold.htm>

Bibliography of Samuel Aughey

1.   (1861) *The renovation of politics: a discourse delivered in St. Paul's Evangelical Lutheran Church, Lionville, Chester County, PA, on the evening of January 4th, 1861* (West Chester, Pennsylvania: E. F. James, Steam-power Book and Job Printer, 15 pp).

2.   (1872) Modern culture. *The Hesperian Student, University of Nebraska* 2(3): 2.

3.   (1873) Modern culture [continued]. *The Hesperian Student, University of Nebraska* 2(4). [not seen and a copy may no longer exist]

4.   (1873) The rattle of the rattlesnake. *American Naturalist* 7: 85-86.

5.   (1873) *The geology of Nebraska: a lecture delivered in the Representative Hall, at Lincoln, on Thursday evening, January 30th, 1873, before the Senate and House of Representatives by the unanimous request of the Legislature* (Lincoln: State Journal Printing Company, 16 pp).

6.   (1873) Report of the Chemical Department of Nebraska University. In *Nebraska State University Annual Report to the Board of Regents for the Academic Year Ending June 25, 1873*, pp. 13-15 (Lincoln: The State Register Book and Job Print).

7.   (1874) Report of the Chemical Department of the Nebraska State University. In AR Benton (Chancellor), *Chancellor's report to the Board of Regents for the academic year, ending June 24th, 1874*, pp. 29-31 (Lincoln: Journal Company, State Printers).

8.   (1875a) *Catalogue of the flora of Nebraska* (Lincoln: University of Nebraska, Southwestern Printing Company, 37 pp).

9.   (1875b) Grasshoppers. *Western Nebraskan*, North Platte, p. 1, 28 May.

10. (1875c) Report of the Department of Natural and Physical

Sciences. In AR Benton, (Chancellor), *The Chancellor's report for the fourth session of the University of Nebraska, ending June 23d, 1875,* pp. 27-30 (Lincoln: Journal Company, State Printers).

11. (1875d) Surface geology of the Platte Valley. *The Pioneer* 2/3:1.

12. (1876a) The superficial deposits of Nebraska. In FV Hayden (Editor), *U. S. Geological and Geographical Survey of the Territories,* Eighth Annual Report, pp. 243-269 (Washington, DC: Government Printing Office).

13. (1876 [1875]b) The surface geology of Nebraska. In EA Curley (Author), *Nebraska; its advantages, resources, and drawbacks,* pp. 114-139 (London, UK: Sampson Low, Marston, Low and Searle, 433 pp).

14. 1(876 [1875]c) The wild fruit of Nebraska. In EA Curley (Author), *Nebraska; its advantages, resources, and drawbacks,* pp. 316-335 (London, UK: Sampson Low, Marston, Low and Searle, 433 pp).

15. (1876d) [Letter concerning Rocky Mountain locust]. In CV Riley (Author), *Eighth Annual report on the noxious, beneficial, and other insects of the State of Missouri,* p. 114 (Jefferson City, Missouri: Regan & Carter, Printers and Binders). [Reprinted in Riley 1878b: 245]

16. (1876e) Report of the Department of Natural and Physical Sciences. In AR Benton (Chancellor), *The Chancellor's Report to the Board of Regents for the year ending June 22d, 1876,* pp.14-17 (Lincoln: Journal Company, State Printers).

17. (1876f) Fossil camels. *The Nebraska State Journal,* Lincoln, p. 4, 24 June.

18. (1876g) *Nebraska.* (Philadelphia, Pennsylvania: Nebraska's Centennial Offering, 16 pp).

19. (1876h) *A appeal for the insane poor in the county poor-houses in Pennsylvania* (Harrisburg, Pennsylvania: Wills Eye Hospital Philadelphia and Obstetrical Society of Philadelphia, 11 pp).

[fourth author with J Curwen, I Ray, JS Billings, LH Steiner, and JV Shoemaker]

20. (1876i) Our insect enemies. *Omaha Daily Republican* 19(149): 2, 12 December.

21. (1877a). Our danger and our remedy from insects. *Nebraska Farmer* 1(1): 7-8, 1 January.

22. (1877) Nebraska apples at the centennial. *Nebraska Farmer* 1(1): 10-11, 1 January.

23. (1877) A plea for the birds. *Perry Daily Chief,* Perry, IA, p. 1, 25 January.

24. (1877) The present condition of the locusts in Nebraska. *The Nebraska State Journal,* Lincoln, p. 2, 30 May. [second author with Cyrus Thomas]

25. (1877) Intellectual advantages of farm life. *Nebraska Farmer* 1(6): 4, 1 June.

26. (1877) Catalogue of the land and fresh-water shells of Nebraska. *Bulletin of the U. S. Geological and Geographical Survey of the Territories* 3(3): 697-704.

27. (1877) The grasshoppers of Nebraska: report of the Entomological Commission to Governor Garber. *Nebraska State Journal,* Lincoln, p. 4, 20 June. [second author with Cyrus Thomas] [Reprinted in Riley 1878b: 12-13]

28. (1877) Fremont and the birds. *Nebraska Farmer* 1(7): 5, 1 July.

29. (1877) The Popular Science Monthly. *Nebraska Farmer* 1(7): 6, 1 July.

30. (1877) The cow birds. *Nebraska Farmer* 1(7): 6, 1 July.

31. (1877) Schuyler and Colfax County. *Nebraska Farmer* 1(9): 6, 1 September.

32. (1877) The increasing need for forests. *Nebraska Farmer* 1(10): 8, 1 October.

33. (1877) What forest tree culture needs. *Nebraska Farmer* 1(12): 7-8, 1 December.

34. (1877) [Note: Numerous Streams in Nebraska]. In RW Furnas (Editor), *Transactions of the Nebraska State Horticultural Society for the year 1877*, p. 9 (Lincoln: Journal Company, State Printers, 125 pp).

35. (1877) Bird and insect talk [Aughey's comments in published discussion of topic]. In RW Furnas (Editor), *Transactions of the Nebraska State Horticultural Society for the year 1877*, pp. 99, 101, 105, 109 (Lincoln: Journal Company, State Printers, 125 pp).

36. (1878) The character of the people of Nebraska. *Nebraska Farmer* 2(2): 24, 1 February.

37. (1878) The buffalo berry. *Nebraska Farmer* 2(4): 54-55, 1 April.

38. (1878) The new coal mine. *Nebraska Herald*, Plattsmouth, p. 2, 4 April.

39. (1878) Artificial stone. *Columbus Era*, Columbus, p. 3, 27 April.

40. (1878) [Note: Size of swarm of Rocky Mountain Locust]. In CV Riley (Editor), *First annual report of the United States Entomological Commission for the year 1877 relating to the Rocky Mountain Locust*, p. 160 (Washington, DC: Government Printing Office, 477 + [295] pp).

41. (1878) Some facts and considerations concerning the beneficial work of birds. In CV Riley (Editor), *First annual report of the United States Entomological Commission for the year 1877 relating to the Rocky Mountain Locust*, pp. 338-350 (Washington, DC: Government Printing Office, 477 + [295] pp).

42. (1878) [Letter to Prof. Cyrus Thomas, United States Entomological Commission, 15 November 1877]. In CV Riley (Editor), *First annual report of the United States Entomological Commission for the year 1877 relating to the Rocky Mountain Locust*, Appendix II, p. [13] (Washington, DC: Government Printing Office, 477 + [295] pp).

43. (1878) Notes on the nature of the food of the birds of Nebraska. In CV Riley (Editor), *First annual report of the United States Entomological Commission for the year 1877 relating to the Rocky Mountain Locust,* Appendix II, p. [14]-[62] (Washington, DC: Government Printing Office, 477 + [295] pp).

44. (1878) Nebraska data for 1877. In CV Riley (Editor), *First annual report of the United States Entomological Commission for the year 1877 relating to the Rocky Mountain Locust,* Appendix VIII, pp. [117]-[133] (Washington, DC: Government Printing Office, 477 + [295] pp).

45. (1878) Economical and superficial geology of Nebraska. In LD Burch (Author), *Nebraska as it is. Resources, advantages and drawbacks, of the Great Prairie State,* pp. 39-55 (Chicago: C. S. Burch & Co., Publishers, 164 pp).

46. (1878) The western locust or grasshopper—its visits no longer feared. *Nebraska Reporter,* Seward, p. 4, 12 December.

47. (1878) Course and character of emigrants, and what per cent is available to the Lutheran Church. *The Lutheran Quarterly* (new series) 8: 382-395.

48. (1879) Forest culture in Nebraska. *Omaha Herald,* Omaha, p. 2, 21 March.

49. (1879) Ancient Nebraska buffaloes. *Saline County Union,* Crete, p. 1, 9 May.

50. (1879) Relations of insects to horticulture and agriculture. In RW Furnas (Editor), *Annual reports of the Nebraska State Horticultural Society, 1878 and 1879,* pp. 96-98 (Lincoln: Journal Company, State Printers, 150 pp).

51. (1880a) *Sketches of the physical geography and geology of Nebraska* (Omaha: Daily Republican Book and Job Office, 326 pp). [quoted extensively by Wilber 1881b; quoted and paraphrased by Florence et al. 1883]

52. (1880b) Nebraska lands west of the One hundredth Meridian. In *Agriculture beyond the 100th Meridian or A Review of the U. S. Public Land Commission* [address to Hon. MW Dunham, President Nebraska Agricultural Society, and Hon. RW Furnas, President Nebraska State Horticultural Society] (Lincoln: Journal Company, State Printers, 7 pp). [first author with CD Wilber]

53. (1880c) Badlands. In H Johnson (Author), *Johnson's history of Nebraska*, pp. 74-75 (Omaha: Herald Printing House).

54. (1880d) Soil. In H Johnson (Author), *Johnson's history of Nebraska*, pp. 76-79 (Omaha: Herald Printing House).

55. (1881a) *The ideas and the men that created the University of Nebraska* (Lincoln: Journal Company, State Printers, 23 pp). [Reprinted in Andreas 1882: 1045-1047.]

56. 1881b. [Letter to Robert W. Furnas and Martin Dunham, 8 February 1880]. In CD Wilber (Author), *The great valleys and prairies of Nebraska and the Northwest*, pp.168-172 (Omaha: Daily Republican Print, 382 pp). [first author with C. D. Wilber]

57. (1881? [1921]) Life on the plains. In TE Sedgwick (Editor), *York County Nebraska and its people, together with a condensed history of the state*, vol. 1, pp. 66-69 (Chicago: S. J. Clarke Publishing Company). [seen only in reprint, original probably printed in 1881 not found]

58. (1882a) Geology. In AT Andreas (Author and Editor), *History of the state of Nebraska; containing a full account of its growth from an uninhabited territory to a wealthy and important state; of its early settlements rapid increase in population, and the marvellous development of its great natural resources. Also an extended description of its counties, cities, towns and villages, their advantages, industries, manufactures and commerce; biographical sketches, portraits of prominent men and early settlers; views of residences and business blocks, cities and towns*, pp. 58-77 (Chicago: The Western Historical Company, 1506 pp).

59. (1882b) Physical and natural features. In AT Andreas (Author and Editor), *History of the state of Nebraska; containing a full account of its growth from an uninhabited territory to a wealthy and important state; of its early settlements rapid increase in population, and the marvellous development of its great natural resources. Also an extended description of its counties, cities, towns and villages, their advantages, industries, manufactures and commerce; biographical sketches, portraits of prominent men and early settlers; views of residences and business blocks, cities and towns*, pp. 78-97 (Chicago: The Western Historical Company, 1506 pp).

60. (1882c) Artesian wells upon the Great Plains; being the report of the geological commission appointed to examine a portion of the Great Plains east of the Rocky Mountains, and report upon the localities deemed most favorable for experimental borings. *Departmental Report, Department of Agriculture, Government Printing Office, Washington, DC* 19: 1-38. [second author with CA White and H Beach]

61. (1882d) Preliminary report on the petroleum basins of Wyoming. In SE Rogers (President), *Report of the Wyoming oil springs: property of the Rocky Mountain Oil, Mining and Transportation Company*, pp. 3-16 (Omaha: John D. Mortimer Printer, 61 pp. + map).

62. (1882e) The North Loup Valley. *The Ord Weekly Quiz*, Ord, p. 4, 13 July.

63. (1883) Improvement of western pasture-land. *Science* 1: 335.

64. (1883) Notes of New Mexico: the cause of stagnation--the advancement of civilization. *The Nebraska State Journal*, Lincoln, p. 6, 7 July.

65. (1883) Opening day for the Tertio Millenial. *The Nebraska State Journal*, Lincoln, p. 7, 7 July.

66. (1883) Mines and mining in New Mexico. *The Nebraska State Journal*, Lincoln, p. 6, 24 July.

67. (1883) Modern Aztecs. *The Nebraska State Journal*, Lincoln, p. 7, 27 July.

68. (1884) Nebraska. In TS Baynes (Editor), *The Encyclopædia Britannica: a dictionary of arts, sciences, and general literature*, pp. 315-319 (Philadelphia: J. M. Stoddart Co., Ltd., ninth edition [American reprint], 17: 1-993).

69. (1884) Curious companionship of the coyote and badger. *American Naturalist* 18: 644-645.

70. (1884) Preliminary statement on the oil properties, owned by the Central Association of Wyoming. In *Petroleum, Coal, Iron, Soda, Land, Central Association of Wyoming*, pp. 7-22 (New York/ Cheyenne: Central Association of Wyoming, 31 pp).

71. (1884) More about beavers. *Popular Science Magazine* 24: 267-268.

72. (1886) *Annual report of the Territorial Geologist to the Governor of Wyoming* (Laramie: Boomerang Printing House, 61 pp).

73. (1890) Nebraska. In DO Kellogg (Editor), *The Encyclopædia Britannica: a dictionary of arts, sciences, and general literature*, pp. 306-309 (New York: The Henry G. Allen Co., ninth ed. [American reprint], 17: 1-858).

74. (1901) S. Aughey's report: oil geologist's favorable opinion of the fields. *Spokesman Review*, Spokane, WA, p. 7, 16 January.

75. (1901). S. Aughey's report: rest of the expert opinion on Rosalia oil fields. *Spokesman Review*, Spokane, WA, p. 7, 17 January.

76. (1902) Prof. S. Aughey's report: incorporated to develop the natural gas fields recently discovered in Whitman County, Washington. In OB Hollis (President), *Prospectus of the Spokane Natural Gas, Oil and Coal Co.*, pp. 6-21 (Spokane: Spokane Natural Gas, Oil and Co., Inland Printing Co., 26 pp).

77. (1906) *Bortle Cooper-Gold Company prospectus in brief and engineer's report* (Detroit: Bortle Copper-Gold Company, 25 pp). [first author with CE Bortle]